Lectures on the
Epistle to the Romans

LECTURES

on the

EPISTLE to the ROMANS

By H. A. Ironside

**Author of "Mysteries of God;" "Minor Prophets;"
"Praying in the Holy Spirit;" "The Four Hundred Silent Years;"
"Lectures on Daniel;" "Lectures on the Revelation," etc., etc.**

LOIZEAUX BROTHERS, Inc.

Neptune, New Jersey

FIRST EDITION, 1928
TWENTY-FOURTH PRINTING, APRIL 1981

Published by LOIZEAUX BROTHERS, Inc.

*A Nonprofit Organization, Devoted to the Lord's Work
and to the Spread of His Truth*

ISBN 0-87213-386-9
PRINTED IN THE UNITED STATES OF AMERICA

FOREWORD

The present volume consists of Notes of Lectures on the Roman Letter, substantially as given to the students of the Moody Bible Institute of Chicago, Ill., the Evangelical Theological College of Dallas, Tex., and at various Bible Conferences through the United States and Canada in recent years.

They are sent forth in printed form in response to the earnest solicitation of many who heard them; and in the hope that they will be used of God to the blessing of numbers who cannot be reached by the spoken word.

The author is indebted far more than he realizes to writers and speakers who have gone over the same ground before him. No claim is made for originality. It is God's truth—not that of any teacher—and as such it is committed to His care for His glory.

H. A. IRONSIDE.

July 30th, 1927.

CONTENTS

LECTURES ON ROMANS

The Righteousness of God Revealed in the Gospel
Chapters 1-8

LECTURE I
The Theme and Analysis

The Epistle to the Romans is undoubtedly the most scientific statement of the divine plan for the redemption of mankind that God has been pleased to give us. Apart altogether from the question of inspiration we may think of it as a treatise of transcendant, intellectual power, putting to shame the most brilliant philosophies ever conceived by the minds of men.

It is noteworthy that the Holy Spirit did not take up an unlettered fisherman or provincial Galilean to unfold His redemption plan in all its majesty and grandeur. He selected a man of international outlook: a Roman citizen, yet a Hebrew of the Hebrews; a man whose education combined familiarity with Greek and Roman lore,

including history, religion, philosophy, poetry,
science and music, together with closest acquaintance with Judaism both as a divine revelation and
as a body of rabbinical traditions and additions to
the sacred deposit of the LAW, the PROPHETS,
and the PSALMS. This man, born in the proud
educational centre, Tarsus of Cilicia, and brought
up at the feet of Gamaliel in Jerusalem, was the
chosen vessel to make known to all nations for
the obedience of faith, the gospel of the glory of
the blessed God, as so marvelously set forth in
this immortal letter.

It was evidently written somewhere along the
journey from Macedonia to Jerusalem, and very
likely, as tradition asserts, at Corinth.

About to leave Europe for Palestine to carry to
the Jewish Christians, his brethren after the
flesh and in the Lord, the bounty provided by the
Gentile assemblies, his heart turns longingly to
Rome, the "eternal city," the mistress of the ancient world, where already apart from direct
apostolic ministry a Christian church had been
formed. To a number of its members he was already known, to others he was a stranger, but he
yearned over them all as a true father in Christ,
and earnestly desired to share with them the
precious treasure committed to him. The Spirit
had already indicated that a visit to Rome was in
the will of God for him, but the time and circumstances were hidden from him. So he wrote this

exposition of the divine plan, and sent it on by a godly woman, Phebe, a deaconess of the assembly at Cenchrea, who had been called to Rome on business. The letter served the double purpose of introducing her to the Christians there and ministering to them the marvelous unfolding of the righteousness of God revealed in the gospel in accordance with the testimony committed to Paul. Think of the grace that entrusted this matchless epistle to the feeble hand of a woman in times such as those! The whole Church of God throughout the centuries owes to Phebe a debt of gratitude, and to the God who watched over her unending praise, for the preservation of the valuable manuscript which she delivered safely into the hands of the elders at Rome, and through them to us.

The theme of the Epistle is the Righteousness of God. It forms one of an inspired trio of expositions which together give us an amazingly rich exegesis of a very brief Old Testament text. The text is found in Habakkuk, chapter 2, verse 4: "The just shall live by his faith." As quoted three times in the New Testament there are just six words, the pronoun "his" being omitted. The three letters referred to are Romans, Galatians, and Hebrews, each of which is based upon this text.

Romans has to do particularly with the first two words. Its message is, "THE JUST shall live by faith," answering the question that is raised in the book of Job, "How shall man be just with God?"

Galatians expounds the two central words, "The just SHALL LIVE by faith." The Galatian error was in supposing that while we begin in faith, we are perfected by works. But the apostle shows that we live by that same faith through which we were justified. "Having begun in the Spirit, are ye now made perfect by the flesh?"

Hebrews takes up the last two words, "The just shall live BY FAITH." It emphasizes the nature and power of faith itself, by which alone the justified believer walks. Incidentally, this is one reason why, after having carefully examined many arguments against the Pauline author-ship of Hebrews, I have not the slightest doubt that it is correctly attributed to the same one who wrote Romans and Galatians; and this is confirmed by the testimony of the apostle Peter, in his second epistle, chapter 3: 15, 16, for it was to converted Hebrews Peter was addressing himself and to them Paul had also written.

The epistles to the Romans may be readily di-vided into three great divisions. Chaps. 1-8 are DOCTRINAL, and give us THE RIGHTEOUS-NESS of GOD REVEALED IN THE GOSPEL. Chaps. 9-11 are DISPENSATIONAL, and give us THE RIGHTEOUSNESS OF GOD HARMONIZED

WITH HIS DISPENSATIONAL WAYS. Chaps.
12-16 are PRACTICAL, and set forth THE
RIGHTEOUSNESS OF GOD PRODUCING
PRACTICAL RIGHTEOUSNESS IN THE BE-
LIEVER. Each of these divisions will be found
to break naturally into smaller subdivisions, and
these into sections and subsections.

In submitting the following outline I do so only
suggestively. The careful student may think of
more apt designations for each particular part,
and may possibly find it simpler to separate the
different paragraphs according to some other ar-
rangement, but I suggest the following analysis
as one that seems to me to be simple and illuminating:

DIVISION I. DOCTRINAL, chaps. 1-8: The Righteousness of God Revealed in the Gospel.

SUBDIVISION I. Chaps. 1: 1—3: 20: The need of the
Gospel.

Section A. Chap. 1: 1-7: Salutation.

Section B. Chap. 1: 8-17; Introduction.

Subsection (a) vers. 8-15: The Apostle's Steward-
ship.

Subsection (b) vers. 16, 17: The Theme Stated.

Section C. Chaps. 1: 18—3: 20: The Ungodliness and
Unrighteousness of the entire Human Family Demonstrated, or, The Need of the Gospel.

Subsection (a). Chap. 1: 18-32: The State of the
Degraded Heathen—the Barbarian World.

Subsection (b). Chap. 2: 1-16: The State of the
Cultured Gentiles, the Moralists.

SUBDIVISION I. Chap. 9: God's Past Dealings with Israel in Electing Grace.

SUBDIVISION II. Chap. 10: God's Present Dealings with Israel in Governmental Discipline.

SUBDIVISION III. Chap. 11: God's Future Dealings with Israel in Fulfilment of the Prophetic Scriptures.

DIVISION III. PRACTICAL. Chaps. 12-16: Divine Righteousness Producing Practical Righteousness in the Believer.

SUBDIVISION I. Chaps. 12: 1—15: 7: God's Good, Acceptable, and Perfect Will Revealed.
Section A. Chap. 12: The Walk of the Christian in Relation to his Fellow-believers, and to men of the world.
Section B. Chap. 13: The Christian's Relation to Worldly Governments.
Section C. Chap. 14: Christian Liberty and Consideration for Others.
Section D. Chap. 15: 1-7: Christ, the Believer's Pattern.

SUBDIVISION II. Chap. 15: 8-33: Conclusion.

SUBDIVISION III. Chap. 16: 1-24. Salutations.

APPENDIX. Chap. 16: 25-27: Epilogue: The Mystery Revealed.

I would earnestly press upon the student the importance of committing to memory, if possible, this outline, or some similar analysis of the epistle, before attempting the study of the letter itself. Failure to get the great divisions and subdivisions firmly fixed in the mind leaves the door open for false interpretations and confused views later on. Many, for instance, through not observing that the question of justification is settled in Chapters 3-5, are greatly perplexed when they come to Chapter 7. But if the teaching of the first chapters referred to be clearly understood, then it will be seen that the man in chapter 7 is not raising again the question of a sinner's acceptance with God, but is concerned about a saint's walk in holiness. Then again, how many a soul has become almost distracted by reading eternal issues into chapter 9, altogether beyond what the apostle intended, and endeavoring to bring heaven and hell into it as though these were here the chief questions at issue, whereas God is dealing with the great dispensational question of His sovereign electing grace toward Israel, and His temporary repudiation of them nationally, while in a special way His grace goes out to the Gentiles. I only mention these instances at this time in order to impress upon each student the importance of having an "outline of sound words" in studying this or any other book of the Bible.

I add an additional suggestion or two. It is good to have "catch-words" sometimes to fix things in the mind. Someone has aptly designated Romans as "The Epistle of the *Forum.*" This, I think, is most helpful. In this letter the sinner is brought into the court room, the forum, the place of judgment, and shown to be utterly guilty and undone. But through the work of Christ a righteous basis has been laid, upon which he can be justified from every charge. Nor does God stop here, but He openly acknowledges the believing sinner as His own son, making him a citizen of a favored race, and owning him as His heir. Thus the challenge can be hurled at all objectors, "What shall we then say to these things? If God be for us, who can be against us?" Every voice is silenced, for "It is God that justifieth," and this not at the expense of righteousness, but in full accord therewith. This view readily accounts for the use of legal and judicial terms, so frequently found in the argument.

A dying sinner was once asked if he would not like to be saved. "I certainly would," he replied; "but," he added earnestly, "I don't want God to do anything wrong in saving me." It was through the letter to the Romans he learned how "God can be just and the Justifier of him which believeth in Jesus." You will remember how Socrates expressed himself five hundred years before Christ. "It may be," he said, addressing himself to Plato, "that the Deity can forgive sins, but I do not see how." It is this that the Holy Spirit takes up so fully in this Epistle. He shows us that God does not save sinners at the expense of His righteousness. In other words, if saved at all, it will not be because righteousness has been set aside in order that mercy might triumph; but mercy has found a way whereby divine righteousness can be fully satisfied and yet guilty sinners justified before the throne of high heaven.

The apostle John suggests the same wondrous truth when in his first epistle, chapter 1, verse 9, he says, "If we confess our sins He is faithful and just to forgive us our sins and to cleanse us from all unrighteousness." How· much more natural the sense would seem to our poor minds before being divinely instructed, if it read, "He is merciful and gracious to forgive." Although the gospel is in the most marvelous way the unfolding of the mercy of God, and exalts His grace as nothing else can, yet it is because it rests on a firm foundation of righteousness that it gives such settled peace to the soul who believes it. Since Christ has died, God could not be faithful to Him nor just to the believing sinner if He still condemned the one who trusts in Him who bore our sins in His own body on the tree.

It is, therefore, the righteousness of God that is magnified in this Epistle to the Romans, even as David of old cried, "Save (or deliver) me in Thy righteousness." It was as Luther was meditating on this verse that light began to dawn upon his darkened soul. He could understand how God could damn him in His righteousness, but it was when he saw that God can save in righteousness that his soul entered into peace. And untold myriads have found the same deliverance from perplexity when through this glorious unfolding of the righteousness of God as revealed in the gospel, they saw how "God can save, yet righteous be." If we fail to see this as we study the epistle, we have missed the great purpose for which it was given of God.

I would add one other thought, which I believe is of moment, particularly for those who seek to present the gospel to others. It is this: In Romans, we have the gospel taught to saints, rather than the gospel preached to unsaved sinners. I believe it is very important to see this. In order to be saved it is only necessary to trust in Christ. But in order to understand our salvation, and thus to get out of it the joy and blessing God intends to be our portion, we need to have the work of Christ unfolded to us. This is what the Holy Spirit has done in this precious epistle. It is written to people who are already saved to show them the secure foundation upon which their salvation rests: namely, the righteousness of God. When faith apprehends this, doubts and fears are gone and the soul enters into settled peace.

LECTURE II

Salutation and Introduction

Chapter 1: 1-17.

As we come to a verse-by-verse examination of this epistle, we may well remind ourselves once more of the precious truth that "All scripture is God-breathed and profitable."* God has spoken through His Word, and this letter contains some of the most important messages He has ever given to mankind. It will be well for us, therefore, to approach the study of it in a prayerful and self-judged spirit, putting all our own preconceived ideas to one side and letting God through the inspired Word correct our thoughts, or, better still, supplant them with His own.

The first seven verses, as we have already noticed, form the salutation, and demand a careful examination. Some most precious truths are here communicated in what might seem a most casual manner. The writer, Paul, designates himself a servant, literally, bondman, of Jesus Christ. He does not mean, however, that his was a service of bondage, but rather the whole-hearted obedience of one who realized that he had been "bought with a price," even the precious blood of Christ.

---

*Literal rendering of 2 Tim. 3:16.

There is a story told of an African slave whose
master was about to slay him with a spear, when
a chivalrous British traveler thrust out his arm
to ward off the blow, and it was pierced by the
cruel weapon. As the blood spurted out he demanded the person of the slave, saying he had
bought him by his suffering. To this the former
master ruefully agreed. As the latter walked
away, the slave threw himself at the feet of his
deliverer, exclaiming, "The blood-bought is now
the slave of the son of pity. He will serve him
faithfully." And he insisted on accompanying his
generous deliverer, and took delight in waiting
upon him in every possible way.

Thus had Paul, thus has each redeemed one, become the bondman of Jesus Christ. We have
been set free to serve, and may well exclaim with
the Psalmist, "O Lord, truly I am Thy servant; I
am Thy servant and the son of Thine handmaid:
Thou hast loosed my bonds" (Ps. 116:16).

Not only was Paul in the general sense a servant, but he was a servant of peculiar and exalted
character. He was a called apostle; not as in the
Authorized Version, "called *to be* an apostle."
The words "to be" are in italics and are not required to complete the sense. It may seem a small
thing to which to call attention, but the same
interpolation occurs in verse 7, where it is altogether misleading, as we shall see when we come
to consider it.

We need not think of Paul as one of the twelve. Some question the regularity of the appointment of Matthias, but it seems to me we may well consider his selection by casting lots as the last official act of the old economy. It was necessary that one who had kept company with the Lord and His disciples from the baptism of John should fill the place which Judas had forfeited. Thus the number of the twelve apostles of the Lamb who are (in the glorious days of earth's regeneration which we generally call the Millennium) to sit upon twelve thrones judging the twelve tribes of Israel, would be completed. Paul's ministry is of a different character. He was pre-eminently the apostle to the Gentiles, and to him was committed the special "dispensation of the mystery." This puts his apostleship on an altogether different plane from that of the twelve. They knew Christ on earth, and their ministry in a very definite way was linked with the kingdom and the family of God. Paul knew him first as the glorified Lord Jesus, and his was distinctively the gospel of the glory.

He was "separated unto the gospel of God." We may rightfully think of this separation from several different viewpoints. He had been set apart for his special ministry before his birth. As in the instances of Moses, Jeremiah, and John the Baptist, he was separated from his mother's womb (Gal. 1:15). But he must first learn the weakness

and unprofitableness of the flesh. Then God had
mercy on him, and he was separated from the
Christless mass and called by divine grace. But
there was more than this. He was in a peculiar
sense delivered from both the people of Israel and
the Gentile nations to be a minister and witness of
the things he had seen and heard. And lastly,
he was separated with Barnabas for the specific
work of carrying the gospel to the Gentiles, when
at Antioch in Pisidia, the brethren, in accordance
with the divine command, laid their hands upon
them and sent them away to carry the gospel to
the regions beyond. This gospel is here called
"the gospel of God." In verse 9 it is called "the
gospel of His Son," and in verse 16, "the gospel of
Christ," although there is a possibility that the
words "of Christ" should be dropped, as they do
not appear in some of the best manuscripts.

Verse 2 is parenthetical and identifies the gospel
with the glad tidings promised in Old Testament
times and predicted by the prophets in the Holy
Scriptures. "To Him give all the prophets witness,
that through His name whosoever believeth in
Him shall receive remission of sins." Timothy
had been taught, from a child, the Holy Scriptures,
and the apostle says that these "are able to make
thee wise unto salvation through faith which is
in Christ Jesus."

This gospel is not a new law. It is not a code of
morals or ethics. It is not a creed to be accepted.

It is not a system of religion to be adhered to.
It is not good advice to be followed. It is a divinely
given message concerning a divine Person, the Son
of God, Jesus Christ our Lord. This glorious Being is true Man, yet very God. He is the Branch
that grew out of the root of David, therefore true
Man. But He is also the Son of God, the virgin-
born, who had no human father, and this His
works of power demonstrate. To this blessed fact
the Spirit of Holiness bare witness when He raised
dead persons to life. The expression, "By the resurrection from the dead," is literally, "By resurrection of dead persons." It includes His own
resurrection, of course: but it also takes in the resurrection of the daughter of Jairus, of the
widow's son, and of Lazarus. He who could thus
rob death of its prey was God and man in one
blessed, adorable Person, worthy of all worship
and praise, now and for evermore.

From Him, the risen One, Paul had received
grace (not only unmerited favor, but favor
against merit, for he had deserved the very opposite) and apostleship by divine call, that he
might make known the gospel unto all nations, to
the obedience of faith for Christ's name's sake.

His apostleship, therefore, extended to those
who were in Rome. Hitherto he had not been able
to visit them personally, but his heart went out
to them as the called of Jesus Christ, and so he
writes "to all that be in Rome, called saints."

Observe that they were saints in the same way that he was an apostle, namely, by divine call. We do not become saints by acting in a saintly way, but because we are constituted saints we should manifest saintliness.

As is customary in his letters, he wishes them grace and peace from God our Father and the Lord Jesus Christ. Saved by grace in the first place, we need grace for seasonable help all along the way. Having peace with God through the blood of His cross, we need the peace of God to keep our hearts at rest as we journey on toward the eternal Sabbath-keeping that remains for the people of God.

Verses 8-17 are the Introduction, which make clear his reasons for writing.

It is evident that a work of God had begun in Rome a number of years before the writing of this letter, for already the faith of the Christian assembly there was spoken of throughout the whole world, that is, throughout the Roman Empire. There is no evidence whatever that this work was in any sense linked with apostolic ministry. Both Scripture and history are silent as to who founded the church in Rome. Certainly Peter did not. There is not the remotest reason for connecting his name with it. The boast of the Roman Catholic Church that it is founded on Peter as the rock, and that the Roman Bishop is the successor of St. Peter, is all the merest twaddle. We

have no means of knowing whether any apostle
visited Rome until Paul himself was taken there
in chains.

There seems to have been a providential reason
why he was hindered from going there earlier. He
calls God to witness (that God whom he served not
merely outwardly but in his spirit, the inward
man, in the gospel of His Son) that he had never
ceased to pray for those Roman believers since he
first heard of them; and coupled with his petitions
for them was his earnest request that if it was the
will of God he might have the opportunity to
visit them, and a prosperous journey. How differently that prayer was answered from what he
might have expected, we well know; and it gives
us a little idea of the overruling wisdom of God
in answering all our prayers. No man is competent to say what is prosperous and what is not.
God's ways are not ours.

Paul longed to see them, hoping that he might
be used of God to impart unto them some spiritual
gift which would be for their establishment in the
truth. Nor did he think only of being a blessing
to them, but he fully expected that they would be
a blessing to him. Both would be comforted together.

Many times during the past years he had pre-
pared to go to Rome, but his plans had miscar-
ried. He longed to have some fruit there as in
other Gentile cities, for he felt himself to be a

debtor to all mankind. The treasure committed
to him was not for his own enjoyment, but that
he might make it known to others, whether Greeks
or barbarians, cultured or ignorant. And realizing
this he was ready to preach the gospel in Rome
as elsewhere.

When in verse 16 he says, "I am not ashamed
of the gospel of Christ," I understand that he
means far more than people generally attach to
these words. It was not merely that he did not
blush to be called a Christian, or that he was always ready boldly to declare his faith in Christ;
but the gospel was to him a wonderful, because
inspired, scheme for the redemption of mankind,
a divinely revealed system of truth transcending
all the philosophies of earth, which he was ready
to defend on every occasion. It was not, as some
might have supposed, that he had refrained from
visiting Rome because he did not feel competent to
present the claims of Christ in the metropolis of
the world in such a manner that they could not
be answered and logically repudiated by the cultured philosophers who thronged the great city.
He had no fear that they would be able to overthrow by their subtle reasonings that which he
knew to be the only authoritative plan of salvation.
It is beyond human reason, but it is not illogical
or unreasonable. It is perfect because of God.

This gospel had been demonstratively proven to
be the divine dynamic bringing deliverance to

all who put faith in it, whether the religious Jew or the cultured Greek. It was the power of God and the wisdom of God unto salvation. It met every need of the mind, the conscience, and the heart of man, for in it the righteousness of God was revealed faith-wise. This I take to be the real meaning of the somewhat difficult expression translated "from faith to faith." It is really "out of faith unto faith." That is, on the principle of faith to those who have faith. In other words, it is not a doctrine of salvation by works, but a proclamation of salvation entirely on the faith principle. This had been declared to Habakkuk long centuries before when God said to the troubled prophet, "The just shall live by faith."

This is the text of the entire epistle, as we have already seen, and of Galatians and Hebrews likewise.

It gives us the quintessence of the divine plan, It has been the rest of millions throughout the centuries. It was the foundation of what has been designated the Augustinian Theology. It was the key that opened the door of liberty to Martin Luther. It became the battle-cry of the Reformation. And it is the touchstone of every system since, that professes to be of God. If wrong here, they are bound to be wrong throughout. It is impossible to understand the gospel if the basic principle be misunderstood or denied. Justification by faith alone is the test of orthodoxy. But no mind untaught by the Holy Spirit will ever receive it, for it sets the first man aside altogether as in the flesh and unprofitable, in order that the Second Man, the Man of God's counsels, the Lord Jesus Christ, may alone be exalted. Faith gives all honor to Him as the One who has finished the work that saves and in whom alone God has been fully glorified, His holiness maintained, and His righteousness vindicated, and that not in the death of the sinner but in the salvation of all who believe. It is a gospel worthy of God, and it has demonstrated its power by what it has accomplished in those who have received it in faith.

LECTURE III

The Need of the Gospel

Chapters 1: 18—3: 20.

We have seen that the gospel reveals the right-eousness of God. The apostle now proceeds to show the need of such a revelation, and piles proof upon proof, evidence upon evidence, and scripture upon scripture to demonstrate the solemn fact that man has no righteousness of his own, but is both by nature and practice utterly unsuited to a God of infinite holiness whose throne is established on righteousness. This he does in the next section of the epistle, chap 1:18—3:20. In a masterly way he brings the whole world into court and shows that condemnation rests upon all because all have sinned. Man is guilty, hopelessly so, and can do nothing to retrieve his condition. If God has not a righteousness for him his case is ended.

In verses 18 to 32 of the first chapter the case of the barbarian is considered. "The wrath of God is revealed from heaven against all ungodliness and unrighteousness of men who hold the truth in unrighteousness." The first class is the pagan world. The second, those to whom a divine revelation had come. The barbarians and heathen generally are ungodly. They know not the true God and so are "without God in the world." Therefore their behavior is described as ungodliness.

On the other hand, to the Jew had been committed the knowledge of God and a divine code of righteousness. He gloried in this while walking in unrighteousness. He held the truth (as something on which he had a "corner") in unrighteousness. Against both classes the wrath of God is revealed.

The heathen are without excuse. Paganism and idolatry are not steps in human evolution as man advances from slime to divinity. Heathenism is a declension, not an upward reach. The great pagan nations once knew more than they do now. The knowledge of God brought through the flood was disseminated throughout the ancient world. Back of all the great idolatrous systems is pure monotheism. But men could not stand this intimate knowledge of God for it made them uncomfortable in their sins; so a host of lesser deities and divinities were invented as go-betweens, and eventually the knowledge of the true God was entirely lost. But even to-day creation is His constant witness: "That which may be known of God is manifest to them; for God hath showed it to them." This orderly universe with its succession of the seasons and the mathematical accuracy of the movements of the heavenly bodies bears testimony to the Divine Mind. The stars in their courses proclaim the great Creator's power:

> "Forever singing as they shine,
> The Hand that made us is divine."

So, "the invisible things of Him from the creation of the world are clearly seen, being understood by the things that are made, even His eternal power and Godhead." One word in the original is rendered by four words in English: "Things-that-are-made" is *Poima,* and from this we get our word *poem.* Creation is God's great epic poem, every part fitted together like the lines and verses of a majestic hymn. In Ephesians 2:10 we find the same word again. "We are His *workmanship*" —His poem—"created in Christ Jesus unto good works which God hath before ordained that we should walk in them." This is God's greatest poem: the epic of Redemption.

> "'Twas great to call a world from naught;
> 'Twas greater to redeem."

These two wondrous poems are celebrated in Revelation 4 and 5. In chapter 4 the enthroned and crowned saints worship Christ as Creator. In chapter 5 they adore Him as Redeemer.

Pursuing Paul's argument we note in vers. 21-23 that the barbarous nations are without excuse for their present ignorance and bestial condition, "Because that when they knew God they glorified

Him not as God, neither were thankful; but became vain in their imaginations, and their foolish heart was darkened. Professing themselves to be wise they became fools, and changed the glory of the incorruptible God into an image made like to corruptible man, and to birds, and four-footed beasts and creeping things." Observe the downward steps on the toboggan-slide of idolatry—God first thought of as an idealized man, then likened to the birds that soar into the heavens, next to the beasts that prowl over the earth, and finally to serpents and other detestable creeping things, whether reptilian or insectivorous. Even the Egyptian worshipped the serpent and the scarabeus, and yet back of all Egyptian mythology is hidden the original revelation of one true and living God! What degradation does this imply on the part of one of the most enlightened nations of antiquity! And others bear similar marks of declension and deterioration.

Because men gave God up He gave them up. Twice in the verses that follow we read, "God gave them up," first to uncleanness and then to vile affections. Once we are told, "God gave them over to a reprobate mind." The vile immoralities depicted here are the natural result of turning from the Holy One. The picture of heathenism in its unspeakable obscenities is not over-drawn, as any one acquainted with the lives of idolatrous people will testify. The awful thing is that all this vileness and filthiness is being reproduced in modern high society where men and women repudiate God. If people change the truth of God into a lie and worship and serve the creature rather than the Creator, the whole order of nature is violated; for apart from the fear of God there is no power known that will hold the evil desires of the natural heart in check. It is part of the very nature of things that flesh will be manifested in its worst aspects when God gives men up to follow the bent of their unholy lusts.

What a picture of mankind away from Him do we get in the closing verses. Sin and corruption are everywhere triumphant. Righteousness is not to be found when the back is turned on God. Nor are men sensitive about their sins or ashamed of their evil ways, but "knowing the judgment of God, that they which commit such things are worthy of death, not only do the same, but have pleasure in them that do them."

That the apostle's picture of heathenism is still true the following clipping bears witness: "A Chinese Teacher once told a missionary that the Bible could not be so ancient a book after all, because the first chapter of Romans gave an account of Chinese conduct, such as the missionary could only have written after full acquaintance with the people. The mistake was not an unnatural one, but it is a heathen's testimony to the truth of the Bible."

In the first sixteen verses of the next chapter another class is brought into view: it is the world of culture and refinement. Surely among the educated, the followers of the various philosophic systems, will be found men who lead such righteous lives that they can come into the presence of God claiming His blessing on the ground of their own goodness! Certainly there were those who professed to look with disgust and abhorrence upon the vile lewdness of the ignorant rabble, but were their private lives any holier or any cleaner than those whom they so loudly condemned?

It is now their turn to be summoned into court, so to speak, where the apostle fearlessly arraigns them before the august tribunal of "the righteous Lord,who loveth righteousness." "Therefore thou art inexcusable, O man, whosoever thou art that judgest; for wherein thou judgest another thou condemnest thyself; for thou that judgest doest the same things." Philosophy does not preserve its devotee from the indulgence of the flesh. A recognition of the evil is not necessarily power to overcome the evil. Culture does not cleanse the heart nor education alter the nature; and it is against the doer of evil that the judgment of God according to truth will be rendered. To praise virtue while practising vice may enable one to get by with his fellows, but it will not deceive Him who is of purer eyes than to behold iniquity.

Sternly he asks, "Thinkest thou this, O man,

that judgest them which do such things and doest the same, that thou shalt escape the judgment of God? Or despisest thou the riches of His goodness and forbearance and long-suffering; not knowing that the goodness of God leadeth thee to repentance?" Men are inclined to consider that God is condoning their ways, if "sentence against an evil work is not executed speedily," whereas He waits in long-suffering mercy that men may have opportunity to face their sins and own their guilt, thus finding mercy. Instead of doing this, after the hardness and impenitence of their hearts, men, untouched by divine grace, "treasure up unto themselves wrath against the day of wrath and revelation of the righteous judgment of God, who will render to every man according to his deeds."

What a solemn expression is this—"Treasuring up," or storing up, "wrath against the day of wrath!" How apt was the answer of the poor old colored woman who when taunted with the folly of believing in a "lake of fire and brimstone" because "no such an amount of brimstone could be found in one place," exclaimed solemnly, "Ebryone takes his own brimstone wif' him!" Ah, that is it! Each rebel against God, each sinner against light, each violator of his own conscience, carries his own brimstone with him! He is making his own destiny.

Properly, I believe, we should consider verses 7 to 15 as parenthetical, not merely 13 to 15, as indi-

cated in the Authorized Version. In these verses
great principles of judgment are laid down which
should forever silence the caviler who would
charge God with unrighteousness because some
have light and privileges that others do not enjoy.

Judgment will be "according to truth" and "according to deeds." Men will be judged by the light
they have had, not by the light they never knew.
Eternal life is offered to all who "by patient con-
tinuance in well-doing seek for glory, honor and
incorruptibility." (Observe it is not immortality,
but incorruptibility. The distinction is of great
importance, though the two terms are often confounded in the Authorized Version.) If any were
so characterized, it would prove that there was a
divine work in the soul; but where is the natural
man who so lives? Well then, "unto them that
are contentious and do not obey the truth, but
obey unrighteousness," there can but be meted
out in the day of judgment "indignation and
wrath, tribulation and anguish, upon every soul
of man that doeth evil," whether privileged Jew
or ignorant Gentile.

It is not that God will deal in indiscriminate
judgment with all men therefore; but light given
will be the standard by which they are judged.
None can complain, for if one but "follow the
gleam" he will find light enough to guide his steps
and ensure his salvation. If, by the light of nature, men realize their responsibility to their Cre-

ator, He will make Himself responsible to give
them further light unto the salvation of their
souls.

With Him there is no respect of persons. The
greater the privileges, the greater the responsibility. But where privileges are comparatively
few, He regards ignorant men with no less interest and tender compassion than He does those
whose outward circumstances are seemingly
better.

"As many as have sinned without law shall also perish without law, and as many as have sinned
in the law shall be judged by the law." No principle could be sounder. Men are held responsible
for what they know, or might know if they would.
They are not condemned for ignorance unless that
ignorance be the result of the wilful rejection of
light. "Men love darkness rather than light because their deeds are evil."

The parenthetical verses 13 to 15 emphasize the
plain principle already laid down so forcibly.
Judgment is according to deeds. To know the
law and fail to obey it only increases the condemnation. Doers of the law will be justified, if
such there are. But elsewhere we learn that from
this standpoint all would be lost, for "by the deeds
of the law there shall no flesh be justified in His
sight." The Jew prided himself upon being in
possession of the divine oracles and thought this
made him superior to the Gentile nations round

about. But God has not left Himself without witness; to these nations He has given both the light
of conscience and the light of nature. They shew
"the work of the law written in their hearts."
Observe, it is not that the law is written in their
hearts. That is new birth, and is the distinctive
blessing of the New Covenant. If the law were
written there they would fulfil its righteousness.
But the *work* of the law is quite another thing.
"The law worketh wrath." It is a "ministry of
condemnation." And Gentile sinners who never
heard of the Sinaitic code have a sense of condemnation resting upon them when they live in
violation of the dictates of their divinely-implanted conscience which testifies either for or
against them—"accusing or else excusing one another." This is experimental proof that they are
on the ground of responsibility and that God will
be righteous in judging them in that solemn day
when the Man Christ Jesus will sit upon the
august tribunal of the ages and manifest the secret motives and springs of conduct. This, Paul
says is "according to my gospel." He declares
that the Crucified will sit upon the throne at the
last great assize. "God hath appointed a day in
which He will judge the world in righteousness by
that Man whom He hath ordained; whereof He
hath given assurance unto all men in that He
hath raised Him from the dead" (Acts 17:31).

With all that the apostle had written concerning the sinfulness and degeneracy of the Gentiles, whether barbarian or highly civilized, the Jew would be in fullest agreement. They were "dogs," outside of the Abrahamic covenant, "aliens to the commonwealth of Israel." Their judgment was just, for they were the enemies of God and His chosen people. But it was otherwise with the Hebrews. They were the elect of Jehovah, the chosen race to whom God had given His holy law and favored with abundant tokens of His special regard. So they reasoned, forgetting that holding correct doctrine does not avail if practical righteousness be overlooked or disregarded.

The apostle suddenly summons the proud worldly Sadducee and the complacent Pharisee into court, and proceeds to arraign them along with the despised Gentiles. Verses 17 to 29 give us the examination of the chosen people.

"Behold," he exclaims, "thou art called a Jew, and restest in the law, and makest thy boast of God, and knowest His will, and approvest the things that are more excellent (or, triest things that differ; see *margin*), being instructed out of the law; and art confident that thou thyself art a guide of the blind, a light of them which are in darkness, an instructor of the foolish, a teacher of babes, which hast the form of knowledge and of the truth in the law" (vers. 17-20). In these masterly clauses he sums up all their pretensions. And when I say pretensions, I do not mean pre-

tences. These were the things in which they
gloried and they were largely true. God had revealed Himself to this people as to no other, but
they were wrong in supposing that this exempted
them from judgment if they failed to keep His
covenant. He had said long before, "You only have
I known of all the families of the earth; therefore
will I punish you for all your iniquities" (Amos
3:3).

Privilege increases responsibility. It does not, as
they seemed to think, set it aside. The knowledge
of the divine oracles gave to the Jew a standard of
judgment that no others had. Therefore, how
much holier should be his life! Were the Israelites
then a more righteous people than the nations
about them? On the contrary, they failed more
miserably than those of less light and fewer privileges.

Incisively the Spirit of God drives home the
truth as to their actual state, in four questions
calculated to expose the inmost secrets of their
hearts and to lay bare the hidden sins of their
lives. "Thou therefore which teachest another,
teachest thou not thyself?" You are so confident
that you are fitted to instruct the ignorant, have
you heeded the instruction given in the law? No
answer!

"Thou that preachest a man should not steal,
dost thou steal?" Throughout the ancient world
the Jew was looked upon as the arch-thief, using

every cunning device known to the money-lender and usurer to part his clients from their wealth. True, driven by desperation, the Gentile voluntarily put himself into the hand of the Jewish pawnbroker, but he knew as he did so that he was dealing with one who had no niceties of pity or compassion for an indigent debtor when the debtor was a hated Gentile dog. The Jew is again speechless.

"Thou that sayest a man should not commit adultery, dost thou commit adultery?" Lechery of the gravest kind was not an uncommon offence in Israel, as the divine records prove and as history bears witness. The evil is in the very nature of man. Out of the heart proceed fornication, lasciviousness, and every unclean thing. In this respect the Jew is as guilty as his Gentile neighbor. He has no reply.

Perhaps the keenest thrust is in the last question of all. "Thou that abhorrest idols, dost thou commit sacrilege?" The word translated "commit sacrilege" really means "to traffic in idols." This was an offence of which the Jew was peculiarly guilty. Abhorring images, he nevertheless was often known to act as a go-between in disposing of idols stolen from the temples of a conquered people and those ready to purchase them in other districts. He was even charged with systematically robbing temples and then selling the images. The town-clerk of Ephesus had this in mind when he said, "Ye have brought hither these men, which are neither robbers of temples (not, churches), nor yet blasphemers of your goddess" (Acts 19: 37). So this was indeed a home-thrust, exposing at once the hypocritical character of the man who professed detestation of idolatry and all its works, and yet was not above profiting financially at the expense of idolators in a manner so thoroughly dishonest.

So the apostle drives home the tremendous indictment! "For the name of God is blasphemed among the Gentiles through you, as it is written" (ver. 24). This their own prophets had declared, and he but insists upon what Scripture and their consciences confirmed.

To trust in circumcision, the sign of the Abrahamic covenant, while walking in so carnal a manner, was but deceiving themselves. Ordinances do not profit if that of which the ordinance speaks is neglected. The uncircumcised Gentile, if he walk before God in righteousness, will be accounted as circumcised, whereas the covenant-mark on the flesh of a Jew will only add to his condemnation if he lives in opposition to the law.

It is reality that counts with God. The true Jew (and "Jew" is a contraction of "Judah," meaning, "Praise") is not one who is such by natural birth alone, or by outward conformity to ritual, but one who is circumcised in heart, who has judged his sinfulness in the sight of the Lord, and who now seeks to walk in accordance with the revealed will of God. "Whose *praise* (note the play on the word Jew) is not of man but of God" (vers. 26-29).

In chapter 3:1-20 we have the great indictment, the summing up of all that has gone before. There is no moral distinction between Jew and Gentile. All are bereft of righteousness. All are shut up to judgment, unless God has a righteousness of His own providing for them.

That the Jew has certain advantages over the Gentile is acknowledged as self-evident, and of these the chief is the possession of the Holy Scriptures, the oracles of God. But these very Scriptures only made his guilt the more evident. Even if they did not really have faith in these sacred writings yet their unfaith cannot make void the faithfulness of God. He will fulfil His Word even if it be in the setting aside of the people He chose for Himself. He must be true though all others prove untrue. In judgment He will maintain His righteousness, as David confesses in Psalm 51 (vers. 1-4).

Does man's unrighteousness then but prepare the way for God to display His righteousness, and is it a necessity of the case? If so, sin is a part of the divine plan and man cannot be held accountable. But this the apostle indignantly refutes. God is just. He will judge men for their sins in righteousness. And this could not be if sin were foreordained and pre-determined. If the latter were true man might have just cause to complain: "If the truth of God hath more abounded through my lie unto His glory, why yet am I also judged as a sinner?" And in that case what was being slanderously reported by some as the teaching of Paul, "Let us do evil that good may come," would be correct. But all who so plead show themselves deficient in moral principle. Their judgment is just.

Then in verses 9-20 we have the divine verdict on the entire human race. The Jew is no better than the Gentile. All alike are under—that is, slaves to—sin. And this the Old Testament confirms. Like a masterly lawyer he cites authority after authority to prove his case. The quotations are largely from the Psalms, and one from the prophet Isaiah. (See Ps. 14:1-3; 53:1-3; 5:9; 140:3; 10:7; Isa. 59:7,8; Ps.36:1.) These are testimonies the Jew could not attempt to refute, coming as they do from his own acknowledged Scriptures. There are fourteen distinct counts in this indictment or summary of evidence.

1—"There is none righteous, no, not one." All have failed in something.

2—"There is none that understandeth." All have become wilfully ignorant.

3—"There is none that seeketh after God." All seek their own.

4—"They are all gone out of the way." They have deliberately turned their backs on the truth.

5—"They are together become unprofitable." They have dishonored God instead of glorifying Him.

6—"There is none that doeth good, no, not one." Their practices are evil. They do not follow after that which is good.

7—"Their throat is an open sepulchre," because of the corruption within.

8—"With their tongues they have used deceit." Lying and deception are characteristic.

9—"The poison of asps is under their lips." It is the poison inserted into the very nature of man by "that old serpent the devil and Satan" at the very beginning.

10—"Whose mouth is full of cursing and bitterness" for "out of the abundance of the heart, the mouth speaketh."

11—"Their feet are swift to shed blood." Hatred produces murder, and, alas, in how many ways it is manifested!

12—"Destruction and misery are in their ways," because they have forgotten God the source of life and blessing.

13—"The way of peace have they not known," for they have deliberately chosen the ways of death.

14—"There is no fear of God before their eyes."
Hence there is no wisdom in them.

Can any plead "Not guilty" to all of these
charges? If so, let him speak. But none can honestly do so. And so he concludes, "We know that
what things soever the law saith, it saith to them
who are under the law: that every mouth may be
stopped and all the world become **guilty** before
God. Therefore by the deeds of the law there
shall no flesh be justified in His sight, for by the
law is the knowledge of sin" (vers. 19-20).

It is God saying again, as in the days of Noah,
"The end of all flesh is come before Me!" "They
that are in the flesh cannot please God." "The
flesh profiteth nothing." How slow we are to
learn this! How hard it is for the natural man to
give up all pretension to righteousness and to fall
down in the dust of self-judgment and repentance
before God, only to find he is then in the very
place where grace can meet him!

The law was given to a special people as we
have seen. They alone were "under the law." That
Gentiles were not, we have already been told in
chapter 2:12-14. How, then, does the failure of
those under the law bring in all the world as
guilty before God? An illustration may help. A
man has a desert ranch of large extent. He is told
it is worthless as pasturage or farming land. He
fences off twelve acres; breaks it, harrows it, fer-

tilizes it, sows it, cultivates it, and reaps only sage-
brush and cactus! It is no use trying out the rest,
for all is of the same character. He says it is all
good-for-nothing, so far as agriculture is concerned. Israel was God's twelve acres. He gave them
His law, instructed them, disciplined them,
warned them, restrained them, protected them,
and sent His Son to them; and Him they rejected
and crucified. In this act the Gentiles joined. All
are under judgment to God. There is no use of
further test. There is nothing in the flesh for
God. Man is hopelessly corrupt. He is not only
guilty, but is utterly unable to retrieve his condition. The law but accentuates his guilt. It
cannot justify. It can only condemn.

How hopeless is the picture! But it is the dark
background on which God will display the riches
of His grace in Christ Jesus!

LECTURE IV

The Gospel in Relation to our Sins

Chapters 3: 21—5: 11.

It is with a sense of the greatest relief that we turn from the sad story of man's sin and shame to contemplate the wondrous grace of God as told out in the gospel, the divine remedy for the ruin that came in by the fall. And this presentation of the good news is in two parts: it presents the gospel first as having to do with the question of our sins: and then when that is settled, as having to do with our sin; the sin-principle, sin in the flesh, the carnal mind which dominates the unsaved, unregenerated man. The first theme is fully taken up in chapters 3:21 to 5:11, and this we will now consider.

"BUT NOW"—exclaims the apostle. It marks a decided change of subject. *Now* that man has been fully shown up, God will be revealed. *Now* upon the proven unrighteousness of all mankind "the righteousness of God is manifested." Of old He had declared, "I will bring near My righteousness." This is in no sense a wrought-out, legal righteousness, such as man was unable to produce for God. It is a righteousness "without the law," that is, altogether apart from any principle of human obedience to a divinely-ordained code of morals. It is a righteousness of God for unrighteous men, and is in no wise dependent upon human merit or attainment.

The Righteousness of God is a term of wide import. Here it means a righteousness of God's providing—a perfect standing for guilty men for which God makes Himself responsible. If men are saved at all it must be in righteousness. But of this, man is utterly bereft. Therefore God must find a way whereby every claim of His righteous throne shall be met, and yet guilty sinners be justified from all things. His very nature demands that this must not be at the expense of righteousness but in full accord with it.

And this has been in His mind from the beginning. It is "witnessed," or borne testimony to, "by the law and the prophets." Moses depicts it in many types of remarkable beauty. The coats of skin wherein our first parents were clothed; the sacrificial victims accepted in behalf of the offerers; the wonderful symbolism of the Tabernacle; all tell out the story of a righteousness provided by God for the unrighteous sinner who turns to Him in faith. The prophets, too, take up the same story. They predict the coming of the Just One who was to die to bring unjust men nigh to God. "Deliver me in Thy righteousness," cries David. "Purge me with hyssop and I shall be

clean; wash me, and I shall be whiter than snow,"
he prays. "He hath clothed us in the garments
of salvation, in the robe of righteousness," says
Isaiah, for "the chastisement of our peace was
upon Him" who was "bruised for our iniquities."
"This is His name," exclaims Jeremiah, "whereby He shall be called, the Lord our Righteousness." "I will save you from all your unclean-
nesses," is the promise through Ezekiel. To Daniel
the angel Gabriel foretells the making of "reconciliation for iniquity" and the bringing in of
"everlasting righteousness." The so-called Minor
Prophets take up the same strain, and all point
forward to the Coming One through whom salvation will be secured for all who repent; Jehovah's
Fellow, who will become the smitten Shepherd for
man's redemption. "To Him give all the prophets
witness that through His name whosoever believeth in Him shall receive remission of sins"
(Acts 10:43).

The righteousness of God is a "by faith" righteousness. It is not "by works." Faith is taking
God at His word. So He has sent a message to
man to be believed. It is the offer of an unim-
peachable righteousness to all, but is only upon
all them who believe. There is a question as to the
reading here. Some editors reject "and upon all."
But there can be no question of the underlying
truth. God freely offers a righteousness to all.
It is the covering of all those who believe, and

of them only. All need it alike, for all have sinned. There is no difference as to this. No man has come up to the standard. All have come short of the glory of God. But He is not looking for merit in man. He offers His righteousness as a free gift. So we read, "Being justified freely by His grace through the redemption that is in Christ Jesus" (ver. 24).

To be justified is to be declared righteous. It is the sentence of the judge in favor of the prisoner. It is not a state or condition of soul. We are not justified because we have become righteous in heart and life. God justifies first, then He enables the justified one to walk in practical righteousness. We are justified *freely*. The word means "without price!" It is the same as in John 15:25, "They hated me without a cause." There was nothing evil in the ways or life of Jesus, for which men should hate Him. They hated Him *freely*. So there is no good in man for which God should justify him. He is justified freely, *without a cause,* when he believes in Jesus.

This is "by grace." Grace is not only unmerited favor. Grace is favor against merit. It is the goodness of God, not alone to men who have done and can do nothing to deserve it, but it is favor shown to men who have deserved the very opposite. "Where sin abounded, grace did much more abound."

"Sovereign grace, o'er sin abounding;
    Ransomed souls the tidings swell,
'Tis a deep that knows no sounding;
    Who its length and breadth can tell?
        On its glories
    Let my soul forever dwell."

In order thus to show grace in righteousness to admittedly guilty sinners God must have a just and satisfactory basis. Sin cannot be overlooked. It must be atoned for. This has been effectuated "through the redemption that is in Christ Jesus." Redemption is a buying back. Man's life is forfeited because of his iniquitous ways. He is sold under judgment. Christ the Holy One—God and Man in one glorious Person upon whom the violated law had no claim—took the guilty rebel's place, paid the utmost penalty, thus redeeming the believing sinner from the wrath and curse to which he had sold himself.

"He bore on the tree, the sentence for me,
    And now both the Surety and sinner are free."

And He who died lives again and is Himself the abiding propitiation—literally, the mercy-seat, the place where God can meet with man through Christ's atoning blood—available to faith. The apostle clearly alludes to the blood-sprinkled mercy-seat on the ark of the covenant of old. Within the ark were the tables of the law. Above

were the cherubim, "justice and judgment" the
habitation of God's throne. They are ready, as it
were, to leap from that throne to execute God's
righteous wrath against the violators of His law.
But sprinkled upon the mercy-seat is the blood
that typifies the sacrifice of the cross. Justice and
judgment ask no more. "Mercy rejoiceth against
judgment," for God Himself has found a ransom.

Till the Lord Jesus suffered for sins, the Just
for the unjust, to bring us to God, the sin-question was not really settled. "It was not possible
that the blood of bulls and goats should take
away sins." Old Testament saints therefore were
all saved "on credit," as we say. Now that Christ
has died the account is closed, and God declares
His righteousness in pretermitting sins down
through the past ages when men turned to Him
in faith. It is not *our* past sins He refers to in
verse 25. It is the sins of believers in the ages
before the cross. And now God declares *at this
time*—since the work is done—His righteousness,
for He has shown how He can be just and yet
justify ungodly sinners who believe in Jesus.
This leaves no room for boasting on man's part,
rather for shame and contrition in view of what
our sins cost the Saviour, and of joyful praise as
we contemplate the grace that wrought so won-
drously on our behalf. Human merit is barred out
in the very nature of the case. Salvation is
through grace by faith. "Therefore we conclude

that a man is justified by faith apart from the
deeds of the law." This then embraces lawless
Gentiles as well as law-breaking Jews. The same
evangel is for all. He who is the Creator of all
has passed none by. He will justify the circumcised, not by ritual, but by faith, and the uncircumcised Gentile through faith likewise.

Does this invalidate or ignore the law? Not at
all. The law condemned the breaker of it and demanded vengeance. This Christ has borne, so the
majesty of the law is upheld, yet sinners are
saved.

> "On Christ Almighty vengeance fell
> That would have sunk a world to hell;
> He bore it for a chosen race,
> And thus became a Hiding-place."

In chapter four the apostle proceeds to show, by
means of Abraham and David, how all this is witnessed by the law and the prophets. Abraham is
taken from the Pentateuch, the books of the law;
David from the Psalms, which are linked with the
Prophets.

What then do we see in Abraham? Was he
justified before God by his works? If so, he had
this to boast in, that he had righteously deserved
the divine approval. But what does the Scripture
say? In Gen. 15:6 we are told that "Abraham
believed God, and it was counted unto him for

righteousness." This is the very principle the apostle has been pressing and explaining so clearly.

To earn salvation by works would be to put God in man's debt. He would owe it to the successful worker to save him. This is the very opposite of grace, which is mercy shown "to him that worketh not, but believeth on Him that justifieth the ungodly." It is his faith that is counted for righteousness. To this then Abraham bears testimony. And David too is heard singing the blessedness of the man to whom God imputes righteousness without works, when he cries in Psalm 32: "Blessed are they whose iniquities are forgiven, and whose sins are covered. Blessed is the man to whom the Lord will not impute sin." In the psalm the Hebrew word for "covered" means "atoned for." This is the gospel. Atonement has been made. Therefore God does not impute sin to the believer in His Son, but imputes righteousness instead.

Luther called the 32nd Psalm "a Pauline Psalm." It teaches in no uncertain way the same glorious doctrine of justification apart from human merit. The non-imputation of sin is equivalent to the imputation of righteousness. Augustine of Hippo had these words painted on a placard, and placed at the foot of his bed where his dying eyes could rest upon them. To myriads more they have brought peace and gladness in the knowledge of transgression forgiven and sin atoned for, as the Hebrew word in the Old Testament translated "covered" really means.

This blessedness was not—is not—for a chosen few only, but is freely offered to all. Faith was reckoned to Abraham for righteousness when he was on Gentile ground before the covenant sign of circumcision was placed upon his flesh. It was really a seal of what was already true, as in the case of Christian baptism; because he was justified he was commanded to be circumcised. In the centuries since the Jews had come to regard the sign as of more importance than the faith. People ever exalt the visible at the expense of the invisible.

Abraham is called "the father of circumcision," for through him the ordinance began. But he is father not only to them who are of the circumcision literally, but to all who have no confidence in the flesh, who have judged it as weak and unprofitable, and who, like him, trust in the living God.

The promise that he should be heir of the world was not given to him "through the law," that is, it was not a reward of merit, something he had earned by obedience. It was on the ground of sovereign grace. Hence his righteousness, like ours if we believe, was a "by-faith righteousness." The heirs of the promise are those who accept it in the same faith, otherwise it would be utterly invalidated. It was an unconditional promise.

The law promised blessing upon obedience and denounced judgment on disobedience. None have kept it. Therefore, "The law worketh wrath." It cursed. It could not bless. It intensified sin by giving it the specific character of transgression, making it the wilful violation of known law. It could not be the means of earning what was freely given.

The promise of blessing through the Seed— which is Christ—is of faith that it might be by grace. And so it is "sure" to all the seed, that is, to all who have faith. All such are "of the faith of Abraham." He is thus the father of us all, who believe in Jesus. And so the word is fulfilled which said, "I have made thee a father of many nations." This comes in parenthetically. The words, "Before Him whom he believed," properly follow the words, "The father of us all." That is to say, Abraham, though not literally our father by natural generation, is the father of all who believe, in the sight of God. The same faith characterizes them all.

God is the God of resurrection. He works when nature is powerless. He so wrought in the case of Abraham and Sarah, both beyond the time when they could naturally be the parents of a child. He so wrought when He raised up Christ, the true Seed, first by bringing Him into the world contrary to nature, of a virgin mother; and second by bringing Him up from the dead. Abraham believed in the God of resurrection, and staggered not at the divine promise though fulfilment seemed impossible. God delights to do impossibilities! What He promises He performs. Fully persuaded of this, Abraham believed God and it was imputed to him for righteousness. In the same way we are called upon to believe on Him who raised up Jesus our Lord from the dead—He who was, in infinite grace, delivered up to death to make atonement for our offences, and who, upon the completion of His work to God's satisfaction, was raised again for our justification. His resurrection is the proof that God is satisfied. The divine justice has been appeased. The holiness of God has been vindicated. The law has been established. And so the believing sinner is declared justified from all things. Such is the testimony of chapter 4.

In the first eleven verses of chapter 5 we have a marvelous summing up, concluding this phase of the subject. "Therefore," that is, in view of all that has been so clearly established, "being justified by faith we have peace with God through our Lord Jesus Christ." Some would render it, "Let us have peace." But this is to weaken the force of the entire argument. Peace, as used here, is not a state of mind or heart. It is a prevailing condition between two who were once alienated.

Sin had disturbed the relations of Creator and creature. A breach had come in which man could not mend. But peace has been made by the blood of Christ's cross. There is no longer a barrier. Peace with God is now the abiding state into which every believer enters. The sin-question is settled. If two nations be at war there is no peace. If peace is made there is no war. "There is no peace, saith my God, to the wicked." "But Christ has made peace," yea, "He is our peace." We believe it, and we have peace with God.

We might say, "Let us enjoy peace with God." But, "Let us have peace with God," is absurd on the face of it. We have the peace. It is a settled thing. He made it, not we.

" 'Tis everlasting peace,
  Sure as Jehovah's name;
'Tis stable as His steadfast throne,
  Forevermore the same.

"My love is ofttimes low,
  My joy still ebbs and flows,
But peace with Him remains the same,
  No change Jehovah knows.

"I change; He changes not,
  My Christ can never die;
This blood-sealed friendship changes not,
  His truth, not mine, the tie."

"The peace of God" is another thing, as in Phil. 4: 6,7. That is experimental. It is the abiding portion of all who learn to cast every care on Him who is the great Burden-bearer.

To see this distinction and to really grasp it in faith is of prime importance. Until the soul realizes that the peace made by the blood of His cross is eternal and undisturbed, even though one's experience may be very different owing to personal failure or lack of appropriating faith, there will be no certainty of one's ultimate salvation.

But knowing this peace to be based, not on my frames or feelings, but on accomplished redemption, I have conscious access by faith into this grace wherein I stand. I stand in grace; not in my own merit. I was saved by grace. I go on in grace. I shall be glorified in grace. Salvation from first to last is altogether of God, and therefore altogether of grace.

"Grace is the sweetest sound
    That ever reached our ears:
When conscience charged and justice frowned,
    'Twas grace removed our fears.

"Grace is a mine of wealth
    Laid open to the poor,
Grace is the sov'reign spring of health,
    'Tis *life for evermore.*

"Of grace then, let us sing,
   A joyful wondrous theme;
Who grace has brought shall *glory* bring,
   And we shall reign with Him."

This is the golden sceptre held out by the King
of Glory to all who venture to approach in faith.

Note it is *access and standing* that are before
us in this 2nd verse of the 5th chapter of our epis-
tle.   Access is based on standing, not on state.
The terms are to be carefully distinguished.   In
Philippians we read much about "your state."
Paul was greatly concerned about that. He never
had a fear about the standing of the children of
God. That is eternally settled.

Standing refers to the new place in which I am
put by grace as justified before the throne of God
and in Christ risen, forever beyond the reach of
judgment.   State is condition of soul.   It is experience. Standing never varies. State is fluctuat-
ing, and depends on the measure in which I walk
with God.   My standing is always perfect because it is measured by Christ's acceptance. I am
accepted in Him.   "As He is, so are we *in this
world*."   But my state will be good or bad as I
walk in the Spirit or walk after the flesh.

My standing gives me title to enter consciously
as a purged worshiper into the Holiest and to
boldly approach the throne of grace in prayer.
Of old God sternly said, "Stand afar off and wor-

ship." Access was not known under the legal
covenant. God was hidden; the veil was not yet
rent. Now all is different, and we are urged to
"draw nigh with true hearts in full assurance of
faith, having our hearts sprinkled from an evil
conscience, and our bodies washed with pure
water."

"And now we draw near to the throne of grace,
  For His blood and the Priest are there;
And we joyfully seek God's holy face
  With our censer of praise and prayer.
The burning mount and the mystic veil
  With our terrors and guilt are gone;
Our conscience has peace that can never fail,
  'Tis the Lamb on high on the throne."

Thus we do indeed rejoice in the hope of the
glory of God. It is hope—not as uncertainty—but
hope that is sure and certain, because based on
the finished work of the Christ of God and a seat-
ed Priest on the right hand of the Majesty in the
heavens. The glory is assured for all who are
justified by faith, and so have peace with God.

But ere we reach the glory we must tread the
sands of the wilderness. This is the place of test-
ing. Here we learn the infinite resources of our
wonderful God. So we are enabled to glory in tri-
bulations, contrary though these may be to all
that the natural man rejoices in. Tribulation is

the divinely appointed flail to separate the wheat
from the chaff. In suffering and sorrow we learn
our own nothingness and the greatness of the
power that has undertaken to carry us through.
These are lessons we could never learn in heaven.

"The touch that heals the broken heart
   Is never felt above;
His angels know His blessedness,
   His wayworn saints His love."

Thus "tribulation worketh patience" if we accept
it as from our loving Lord Himself, knowing it is
for our blessing. Out of patient endurance springs
fragrant Christian experience, as the soul learns
how wonderfully Christ can sustain in every cir-
cumstance. And experience blossoms into hope,
weaning the heart from the things of earth and
occupying them with the heavenly scene to which
we are hastening.

Thus "hope maketh not ashamed, for the love
of God is shed abroad in our hearts by the Holy
Spirit which is given unto us." This is the first
mention of the Spirit's work in the epistle. We
read of the Spirit of Holiness in chapter one in
connection with Christ's work and resurrection,
but not a syllable about the Spirit's work in the
believer till the soul enters into peace through
the apprehension of the finished work of Christ.
This is all-important. I am not saved by what

goes on within myself. I am saved by what the Lord Jesus did for me. But the Spirit seals me when I believe the gospel, and by His indwelling the love of God is shed abroad within my heart.

> "Soon as my all I ventured
> On the atoning blood,
> The Holy Spirit entered,
> For I was born of God."

It is a great mistake to rely upon my own recognition of the Spirit's work within me as the ground of my assurance. Assurance is by the word of the truth of the gospel. But upon believing, I receive the Spirit. Of this the 8th chapter largely treats. This gives corroborative evidence. "We know that we have passed from death unto life because we love the brethren."

Verses 6 to 11 constitute a separate section. In this portion we have the summing up of all that has gone before, ere the apostle goes on in the next division to take up the second phase of the gospel—in relation to our SIN.

We were helpless, without strength, when God in grace gave His Son, who died for ungodly sinners in whom no merit could be found.

This is not like man. Few indeed could be found who would voluntarily die for an upright man, a righteous man, known and acknowledged to be such—much less for a wicked man. Some indeed might be willing to die for a good man, a kindly, benevolent man who has won their hearts by his gracious demeanor. But God has "commended His own love [see Greek] toward us, in that while we were yet sinners [neither righteous nor good], Christ died for us," thus becoming the Substitute for guilty rebels. If love gave Him up to the death of the cross while we were so lost and vile, we may know beyond any doubt that since we have been justified by His blood He will never allow us to come into judgment: "We shall be saved from wrath through Him."

This has been called the chapter of "the five much mores," and of these we have the first one in the 9th verse. "Much more then," he exclaims, since now, cleared of every charge by the blood of the Son of God, we are forever beyond the reach of the divine vengeance against sin.

The second use of this term is in the 10th verse: "For if when we were enemies, we were reconciled to God by the death of His Son, much more, being reconciled, we shall be saved by His life." How blind are they who read into this a reference to the earthly life of our blessed Lord. That life—pure and holy as it was—could never have saved one poor sinner. It was by His death He made atonement for our sins. Even the love of God told out so fully in the ways of Jesus only drew out the envenomed hate of the human heart. It is His death that destroys the

enmity—when I realize He died for me I am reconciled to God. The hatred was all on my side—
there was no need for God to be reconciled to
me—but I needed reconciliation, and I have found
it in His death. Now since it is already an accomplished fact I may know for a certainty I
"shall be saved by His life." He says, "Because
I live ye shall live also." It is, of course, His resurrection life that is in view. "Wherefore He
is able to save evermore them that come unto
God by Him, seeing He ever liveth to make intercession for them" (Heb. 7: 25, marginal reading). A living Christ at God's right hand is my
pledge of eternal redemption. He lives to plead
our cause, to deliver through all the trials of the
way, and to bring us safely home to the Father's
house at last. We are bound up in the same
bundle of life as Himself, though this properly
is the subject of the last part of the chapter and
has to do with the second phase of salvation.

Secure for time and eternity we "joy in God
through our Lord Jesus Christ, by whom we have
now received the reconciliation" (ver. 11, see margin). It is not we who received the atonement, but God. We needed to make an atonement for our sins, but were unable to do so.
Christ has made it for us by offering up Himself without spot unto God. Thus it is God who
has accepted the atonement, and we, who once
were "enemies" and "alienated in our minds by

wicked works," have received the reconciliation. The enmity is gone. We are at peace with God, and we joy in Him who has become our everlasting portion.

This is the glorious end—for the present—to which the Holy Spirit has been leading us. Our salvation is full and complete. Our sins are gone. We are justified freely by His grace. We have peace with God and we look forward with joyous certainty to an eternity of bliss with Him who has redeemed us.

The other three "much mores" occur in the next section, where the question of the two Headships is thoroughly gone into. We shall notice them in order when we come to them.

LECTURE V

The Gospel in Relation to Indwelling Sin

PART I

Chapters 5: 12—7: 25

It will be necessary to take up this third part of
the great doctrinal division in two lectures because
of the wide scope of chapter 5: 12 to the end of
chapter 8. We shall look first therefore at that
portion which ends with chapter 7. In the last
half of chapter 5 we have the two heads—Adam
and Christ. In chapter 6 we have two masters,
SIN personified and GOD as revealed in Jesus. In
chapter 7 there are two Husbands to be considered—the Law and Christ risen.

The awakened sinner is concerned about one
thing: how to be delivered from the judgment
his sins have righteously deserved. This aspect
of salvation has all been gone into and settled in
the portion we have recently gone over. It is
never raised again. As we go on into this next
part of the epistle the question of guilt does not
come up. The moment a sinner believes the gospel his responsibility as a child of Adam under the
judgment of God is over for ever. But that very
moment his responsibility as a child of God be-

gins. He has a new nature that craves what is divine. But he soon discovers that his carnal nature has not been removed nor improved by his conversion to God, and from this fact arises many trying experiences. It often comes as a great shock, when he realizes that he has still a nature capable of every kind of vileness. He is rightly horrified, and may be tempted to question the reality of his regeneration and his justification before God. How can a Holy God go on with one who has such a nature as this? If he tries to fight sin in the flesh he is probably defeated, and learns by bitter experience what Philip Melanchthon, Luther's friend, put so tersely, "Old Adam is too strong for young Philip."

Happy is the young convert if at this crisis he comes under sound scriptural instruction instead of falling into the hands of spiritual charlatans who will set him to seeking the elimination of the fleshly nature and the death of the carnal mind. If he follows their advice he will be led into a quagmire of uncertainty and dazzled by the delusive will-o'-the-wisp of possible perfection in the flesh, will perhaps flounder for years in the bog of fanaticism and self-torture before reaching the rest that remains for the people of God. I have tried to tell of my own early experiences along this line in a little volume entitled, *Holiness, the False and the True,* which I am thankful to know has been blessed to the deliverance of many thousands of souls. It was the truth we are now to consider that saved me at last from the wretchedness and disappointments of those early years.

In taking up these chapters I desire to antagonize no one but, simply, to constructively open up the line of truth here set forth for the soul's blessing.

And first we have to consider the two great families and the two federal heads of chapter 5: 12-21.

The moment a man is justified by faith he is also born of God. His justification is, as we have seen, his official clearance before the throne of God. His regeneration involves his introduction into a new family. He becomes a part of the New Creation of which the risen Christ is the Head. Adam the first was federal head of the old race. Christ Risen, the Second Man and the Last Adam, is Head of the new race. The old creation fell in Adam, and all his descendants were involved in his ruin. The new creation stands eternally secure in Christ, and all who have received life from Him are sharers in the blessings procured by His cross and secured by His life at God's right hand.

"Joyful now the new creation
 Rests in undisturbed repose,
Blest in Jesus' full salvation,
 Sorrow now nor thraldom knows."

It is the apprehension of this that settles the
question of the believer's security and thus gives
a scriptural basis for the doctrine of deliverance
from the power of sin.

It will be observed that the subject begun in
verse 12 is concluded in verses 18-21. The inter-
vening passage (verses 13-17) is parenthetical,
or explanatory. It may be best therefore for
us to examine the parenthesis first. Sin was in
the world dominating man from Adam's fall
even before the law was given by Moses; but
sin did not as yet have the distinct character of
transgression till a legal code was given to man
which he consciously violated. Therefore, apart
from law, sin was not imputed. Nevertheless
that it was there and to be reckoned with, is
manifest, for "by sin came death" and death
reigned as a despotic monarch over all men from
Adam to Moses, save as God interfered in the
case of Enoch, who was translated that he should
not see death. Even where there was no wilful
sin, as in the case of infants and irresponsible
persons, death reigned, thus proving that they
were part of a fallen race federally involved in
Adam's sin and actually possessing Adam's fallen
nature. He who was originally created in the
image and likeness of God defaced that image by
sin and lost the divine likeness, and we read that
"Adam begat a son in his own likeness, after his
image" (Gen. 5:3). This is characteristic of all

the race of which he is the head. "In Adam all die."

Theologians may wrangle about the exact meaning of all this and rationalists may utterly refuse to accept it, but the fact remains, "It is appointed unto men once to die," and apart from divine interference each one may well say with the poet:

> "I have a rendezvous with death,
> I shall not fail my rendezvous."

You have doubtless heard of the epitaph, often mentioned in this connection, which is engraven on a tombstone marking the resting place of the bodies of four young children in St. Andrew's churchyard in Scotland:

> "Bold infidelity, turn pale and die.
> Beneath this stone four sleeping infants lie:
> Say, are they lost or saved?
> If death's by sin, they sinned, for they are
>   here.
> If heaven's by works, in heaven they can't
>   appear,
> Reason, ah, how depraved!
> Turn to the Bible's sacred page, the knot's
>   untied:
> They died, for Adam sinned; they live, for
>   Jesus died."

There is no other solution to the problem of childhood suffering than that of the fall of the race in Adam.

But Adam was a figure, an antitype, of Him who was to come—yea, who has come and has Himself taken the responsibility of undoing the effects of the fall for all who, trusting in Him, become recipients of His resurrection life; and with this is linked a perfect righteousness which is eternal in duration and divine in origin. There is a difference as to the offence and the gift however. Adam's one offence involved his race in the consequences of his fall. Christ, having satisfied divine justice, offers the gift of life by grace to all who will believe and so it abounds unto many. Notice that here in verse 15 we have the third "much more."

Nor is it merely that as by one that sinned so is the gift—for the one sin brought universal condemnation, putting the whole race under judgment. But the reception of the gift of life and righteousness in faith places the recipient in the position of justification from all things irrespective of the number of offences. Death reigned because of one offence. But we are told that "much more," those who receive this abundance of grace and this free gift of righteousness now reign triumphant over death in life by Jesus Christ, the one who has overcome death and says, "Because I live ye shall live also."

This is the substance of the parenthesis. Now let us go back—with all this in mind—to verse 12, and link it with verses 18-21. Sin entered into the world by one man and death by sin, so death passed upon all men for all have sinned, inasmuch as all were in the loins of Adam when he fell and all the race is involved in the defection of its head.

Now look at verse 18. "Therefore as by one offence" there came universal condemnation, even so by one accomplished act of righteousness on the cross there comes an offer to all—that of justification of life. In other words, a life is offered as a free gift to all who are involved in the consequences of Adam's sin, which is the eternal life manifested in the Son of God who once lay low in death under the sentence of condemnation, but arose in triumph having abolished death, and now as Head of a new race imparts His own resurrection life—a life with which no charge of sin can ever be linked—to all who believe in Him. They share henceforth in a life to which sin can never be in any sense attached. This is a new creation, of which Paul writes so fully in 2 Cor. 5 and in 1 Cor. 15: "If any man be in Christ it is new creation." And it is in new creation that "all is of God"; "Old things have passed away and all things have become new." So we get the full force of the word, "As in Adam all die, so in Christ shall all be made alive."

It is not universal salvation, nor is it merely
that He will raise all the dead, but the two races,
the two creations, the two Headships, are in contrast.   Christ is the beginning, the origin, the
federal Head of the creation of God (Rev. 3:14).
As the risen Man at God's right hand, having
passed through death He now is the fountain of
life, pure, holy, unpolluted life, to all who believe.
So we are now before God in justification of life.

By one man's disobedience the many were constituted sinners. "Much more," by one glorious
act of obedience unto death on the part of Him
who is now our new Head, the many are constituted righteous.

The coming in of the law added to the gravity
of the offence. It gave sin the specific character
of transgression. But where sin abounded (had
reached its flood-tide, so to speak) grace did
"much more abound," that is, grace super-
abounded, so that as sin reigned like a despotic
monarch throughout the long centuries before
the cross, unto the death of all his subjects, now
grace is on the throne and reigns through accomplished righteousness unto eternal life by Jesus
Christ our Lord!

What a gospel! What a plan! It is perfect; it
is divine; like God Himself! How gloriously do
these five "much mores" bring out the marvels
of grace!

In the light of all this, is it any wonder that the apostle, recognizing the innate tendency of the human heart to turn the grace of God into lasciviousness, puts into the mouth of the reader the question, "Shall we continue in sin that grace may abound?" Chapter 6 answers this cavil (for it is really that) in a masterly way.

"Far be the thought!" he exclaims indignantly. "How shall we who have died to sin live any longer therein?" In what sense did we die to sin? If actually dead to it we would not be concerned about either the question or its answer. That which perplexes us is the fact that while we hate sin we find within ourselves a tendency to yield to it. But we are said to have died to it. How and where? The next verses give the answer.

The very fact that our link with Adam as federal head was broken by our association with Christ in His death tells us that we have the right to consider ourselves as having died, in that death of His, to the authority of sin as a master. Israel were redeemed from judgment by the blood of the Lamb. This answers to the first aspect of salvation. By the passage through the Red Sea they died to Pharaoh and his taskmasters. This illustrates the aspect we are now considering. Sin is no longer to hold sway over us, we served it in the past. But death has changed all that. Our condition of servitude is over. We are now linked with Christ risen and thus have been brought to God.

Of this the initiatory ordinance of Christianity speaks. "Know ye not that so many of us have been baptized into (or unto) Christ were baptized into (or unto) His death?" Israel were "baptized unto Moses in the cloud and in the sea." They passed through death in figure, and Moses was their new leader. Pharaoh's dominion was ended so far as they were concerned (1 Cor.10). So we who are saved are now baptized unto, or into, the death of Christ. We have accepted His death as ours, knowing that He died in our place. We are baptized unto Him as the new Leader.

Is this the Spirit's baptism? I think not. The Spirit does not baptize unto death, but into the one new Body. It is establishment into the mystical Christ. Our baptism with water is a baptism unto Christ's death.

The apostle goes further, "Therefore we are buried with Him by baptism unto death; that like as Christ was raised up from the dead by the glory of the Father, even so we also should walk in newness of life" (vs.4). In my baptism I confess that I have died to the old life as a man in Adam under the dominion of sin. I am through with all that. Now let me prove the reality of this by living the life of a resurrected man—a man linked up with Christ on the other side of death—as I walk in newness of life. Thus all thought of living in sin is rejected, all antinomianism refuted. My new life is to answer to the confession made in my baptism.

I am to realize practically my identification with Christ. I have been planted together with Him in the similitude of His death—that is, in baptism—I shall be (one with Him) also in the similitude of His resurrection. I do not live under sin's domination. I live unto God as He does who is my new Head.

Logically he continues, "Knowing this that our old man is crucified with Him, that the body of sin might be destroyed (or, rendered powerless) that henceforth we should not serve sin, for he that is dead is freed (or, justified) from sin" (vers. 6,7).

My old man is not merely my old nature. It is rather all that I was as a man in the flesh, the "man of old," the unsaved man with all his habits and desires. That man was crucified with Christ. When Jesus died I (as a man after the flesh) died too. I was seen by God on that cross with His blessed Son.

How many people were crucified on Calvary? There were the thieves, there was Christ Himself—three! But are these all? Paul says in Gal.2:20, "I am crucified with Christ." He was there too; so that makes four. And each believer can say, "Our old man is crucified with Him."

So untold millions were seen by God as hanging
there upon that cross with Christ. And this was
not merely that our sins were being dealt with,
but that we ourselves as sinners, as children of
Adam's fallen race, might be removed from
under the eye of God and our old standing come
to an end forever.

But we who were crucified with Him now live
with Him. So the apostle continues in Gal.2:20:
"Nevertheless I live, yet not I, but Christ liveth
in me, and the life that I now live in the flesh
(that is, in this body) I live by the faith of the
Son of God who loved me and gave Himself for
me." And so here. The body of sin is thus
annulled, as the body of Pharaoh, all the power
of Egypt, was annulled so far as Israel was concerned. Sin is not my master now. In Christ
I live unto God. I am no longer to be a slave
unto sin. I am righteously free (justified) from
sin's authority.

Now he shows the practical effect of all this
precious truth. We have died with Christ. We
have faith that we shall also live with Him. *Then*
—in heaven—sin will have no authority over us.
Nor should we own its authority here by yielding
ourselves to it. We know that the risen Christ
will never die again. Death's authority (and sin
bringeth forth death) is forever abolished. "In
that He died He died unto sin once for all," unto
sin as our old master (not His—upon Him never

came the yoke, He was ever free from sin), and now in resurrection He lives only unto God. And we are one with Him, therefore we too are henceforth to live unto God alone. This involves practical deliverance from the power or authority of sin.

It certainly never was the mind of God that His blood-redeemed people should be left under the power of the carnal nature, unable to walk in the liberty of free men in Christ. But practical deliverance is not found by fighting with the old master, SIN in the flesh, but by the daily recognition of the truth we have just been considering.

And so we are told to count as true what God considers to be true that we died with Christ to all the claims of Pharaoh-Sin, and we are now free to walk in newness of life as one with Christ risen. "Likewise *reckon* ye also yourselves to be dead indeed unto sin, but alive unto God through Jesus Christ our Lord" (vs.11). This word "Reckon" is one of the key-words of the chapter. It means, literally, "count as true." God says I died with Christ. I am to count it true. God says I live unto Him I count it true. As faith reckons on all this I find the claims of sin are annulled. There is no other method of deliverance than that which begins with this reckoning. Reason may argue, "But you do not feel dead!" What have feelings to do with it? It is a judicial fact. Christ's death

is my death.   Therefore I reckon myself to have
died unto sin's dominion.

The next verse follows in logical sequence.
"Let not sin therefore reign in your mortal body
that ye should obey it in the lusts thereof."   I
feel an impulse rising within demanding that I
yield to a certain sinful desire.   But if on the
alert I say at once, "No, I have died to that.   It
is no longer to dominate my will.   I belong to
Christ.   I am to live unto Him."   As faith lays
hold of this the power of lust is broken.

It involves watchfulness and constant recognition of my union with Christ.   As in times past
I was in the habit of yielding the physical members as instruments of unrighteousness, controlled by sin, now I am to definitely and unreservedly yield myself unto God as one alive from
that death into which I went with Christ, and as
a natural result all my physical members are His
to be used as instruments to work out righteousness for the glory of God whose grace has saved
me.   The word translated "instruments" is really
"weapons," or "armor," as in Chap.13:2; 2 Cor.
6:7 and 10:4. My talents, my physical members,
all my powers are now to be used in the conflict
as weapons for God.   I am His soldier to be
unreservedly at His disposal.

Because I am not saved by any legal principle
but by free grace alone sin is no longer to hold

sway over my life. Christ risen is the Captain
of my salvation whose behests are to control me
in all things.

Nature might reason in a contrary way and
tell me that inasmuch as I am under grace not
law it matters little how I behave, and I am
therefore free to sin since my works have nothing to do with my salvation. But as a regenerated man I do not want liberty to sin. I want power
for holiness. If I habitually yield myself unto sin
to obey its behests voluntarily, I show that I am
still sin's servant, and the end of that service is
death. But as a renewed man I desire to obey
the One whose I now am and whom I serve. So
he says, "God be thanked, that ye were the
slaves of sin, but ye have obeyed from the heart
that form of doctrine which was delivered unto
you. Being then made free from sin (that is,
by God's judicial act on the cross) ye became the
servants of righteousness" (vers.17,18).

He speaks in a figure, illustrating his theme by
personifying SIN and RIGHTEOUSNESS that our
weak human minds may understand, and he repeats his exhortation, or rather what had been
stated doctrinally he now repeats as a command:
"For as ye have yielded your members slaves to
uncleanness and to iniquity unto iniquity (in the
old life before our identification with Christ)
even so now yield your members servants (bondmen) to righteousness unto holiness" (vs.19).

When slaves of sin, righteousness was not our
recognized master, and we can only hang our
heads in shame as we think of the fruit of that
evil relationship, the end of which would have
been death, both physical and eternal.

Therefore now that we are judicially delivered
from sin's dominion and have become bondmen
to God, our lives should be abounding in fruit
unto holiness and the end everlasting life. We
have everlasting life now as a present possession,
but here it is the end that is in view when we are
at home in that scene where Christ who is our
life has gone.

He concludes this section with the solemn yet
precious statement: "For the wages of sin is
death, but the gift of God is eternal life through
Jesus Christ our Lord." Sin is in one respect a
faithful master. His pay day is sure. His wages
are death. Note it is not divine judgment that is in
view for the moment, but sin's wages. Death is the
wages of sin, but "after this the judgment."
Penalty has yet to be faced at the judgment-bar
of God. Through error to see this many have
taken up with the error that physical death involves cessation of being and is both wages and
penalty. Scripture clearly tells of divine judgment after sin's wages have been paid.

On the other hand eternal life is a free gift,
the gift of God. None can earn it. It is given
to all who trust in Christ as the Saviour of sin-

ners. It is ours now, who believe the gospel. We shall enjoy it in all its fulness at the "end."

The seventh chapter takes up another phase of things that would be particularly hard for the Jewish believer to comprehend. It raises and answers the question, "What is the rule of life for the yielded believer?" The Jew would naturally say, "The law given at Sinai." The apostle's answer is "Christ risen!" Alas, how many Gentile believers have missed the point here as well as those who came out of Judaism.

That it is his Jewish-Christian brethren who are primarily before him is clear from the opening verse. "Know ye not, brethren (for I speak to them that know the law), how that the law hath dominion over a man as long as he liveth." Now it is unthinkable that he is using the term "the law" here in any different sense to that which he has had in mind as he has used it over and over again in the former chapters. The law, here, means the law of Moses, and it means nothing else. It means that which was the heart of the law of Moses, the ten words given on Sinai. And his argument here is that the law has dominion over men until death ends its authority or ends their relationship to it. But he has just been showing us in the clearest possible way that we have died with Christ; therefore we died not only unto sin, but we have died to the law as a rule of life. Is this then to leave us lawless? Not

at all: for we are now, as he shows elsewhere
(1Cor.9:21), "under law to Christ", or "en-
lawed", that is, "legitimately subject" to Christ
our new Head. He is Husband as well as Head,
even as Eph.5 so clearly shows.

This truth is illustrated in a very convincing
way in verses 2 and 3, and the application is
made in verse 4. A woman married to a husband
is legally bound to him in that relationship until
death severs the tie. If she marries another
while her husband is living she becomes an adult-
eress. But when the first husband is dead she is
free to marry another with no blame attaching
to her for so doing.

Even so, death has ended the relationship of
the believer to the law, not the death of the law
but our death with Christ, which has brought
the old order to an end. We are now free to be
married to another, even to the risen Christ in
order that we might bring forth fruit unto God.

The somewhat weird and amazing conception
has been drawn from the apostle's illustration
that the first husband is not the law at all but
"our old man." This is utterly illogical and un-
tenable, for, as we have seen, the old man is
myself as a man in the flesh. I was not married
to myself! Such a suggestion is the very height
of absurdity. The Jewish believer was once
linked with the legal covenant. It was proposed
as a means of producing fruit for God. It only

stirred up all that was evil in the heart. Death has dissolved the former relationship, and the one who once looked to the law for fruit now looks to Christ risen and, as the heart is occupied with Him, that is produced in the life in which God can delight.

He says, "When we were in the flesh (that is, in the natural state, as unsaved men) the motions of sins which were by the law, did work in our members to bring forth fruit unto death." This clearly establishes the position taken above. The law was the husband, the active agent through whom we hoped to bring forth fruit unto God. But instead of that, we brought forth fruit unto death, all our travail and suffering in the hope of producing righteousness ended in disappointment, the child was still-born.

"But now we are delivered from the law, having died to that (relationship) wherein we were held (note the marginal reading) that we might serve in newness of spirit, and not in the oldness of the letter" (vs.6). In the illustration the first husband dies and the woman is free to be married to another. In the application he does not say the law has died, but the point he makes is that death (and for us it is Christ's death) has ended the relationship in which we stood toward it. So there is after all no real disagreement; in either case the former condition is ended by death. The law, as we have seen, was addressed

to man in the flesh, and this was our former
state, but now all is changed. We are no longer
in the flesh, but (as the next chapter will show
us) in the Spirit, and so in a new state to which
the law in no sense applies. Again the old question comes to the fore: If all this be true shall
we sin then? Are we to be lawless because not
under law? By no means. The law must simply
be recognized as having a special ministry but
not as the rule of the new life. It is a great
detector of sin. Paul could say, "I had not
known *sin* but by the law." That is, he had not
detected the evil nature within—so correct was
his outward deportment—had not the law said,
"Thou shalt not covet." The sin-nature rebelled
against this and wrought in him all manner of
covetousness, or unsatisfied desire. Observe carefully how conclusively this proves that it was
the ten commandments he has had in view
throughout. To say it is the ceremonial law
alone to which we have died is absurd in view
of this statement. Where is the word found that
forbids covetousness? In the ten commandments.
Therefore "the law" means the divine ordinances
engraved on tables of stone.

Apart from the law sin was dead, that is, inert
and unrecognized. Sins there were even before
the law was given, but sin—the nature—was not
recognized till the law provoked it.

He says, "I was alive once without the law;

but when the commandment came, which was
ordained (or proposed) to life, I found it to be
unto death. For sin, taking occasion by the commandment, deceived me and by it slew me"
(vers. 9-11). In other words it is as though he
said, "I was blissfully unconscious of my true
moral condition before God as a sinner until the
force of the commandment forbidding covetousness came home to me. I had not realized that
evil desire was in itself sinful, providing the
desire was not carried out. But the law made
this manifest. I struggled to keep down all
unlawful desire; but sin—an evil principle within
—was too strong for repression. It circumven-
ted me, deceived me, and so by violation of the
commandment brought me consciously under
sentence of death." This is exactly what the law
was intended to do, as he shows in the epistle to
the Galatians as well as here. "The law was
added because of (or, with a view to) transgres-
sions." That is, the law served to give to sin
the specific character of transgression, thus deep-
ening the sense of guilt and unworthiness.

Therefore, he concludes, "the law is holy, and
the commandment holy, and just, and good."
The fault is not in the law but in me.

Well, then, he asks, was this holy law made
death to me? Not at all, but it detected that in
him which could only result in death—namely,
sin, which in order that it might be made mani-

fest in all its hideousness was brought fully to light by the law, thus "working death" in him by that which he owns to be in itself good. And so sin, by means of the legal enactment, is made exceeding sinful.

Verses 14-25 have been taken by many as the legitimate experience of a Christian throughout all his life. Others have thought that it could not be the conflict of a real Christian at all, but that Paul was describing the conflict between the higher and lower desires of the natural man, particularly of an unconverted Jew under law. But both views are clearly contrary to the argument of this part of the epistle.

As to the latter interpretation, it should be remembered that in this entire section of the epistle the question is the deliverance of a believer from the power of sin, and not of an unbeliever from his sins. Moreover no unsaved man can honestly say, "I delight in the law of God after the inward man." It is only those who possess the new nature who can so speak. And as to this being the normal experience of one already saved I shall attempt to show as we go on with the study of the 7th and 8th chapters that there is an orderly progression from the bewilderment of chapter 7 to the intelligence and walk in the Spirit of chapter 8. All Christians doubtless know something of the state depicted in verses 14-25 of this 7th chapter, but once out of it no one need ever go through it again. It is not merely the conflict between the two natures. If it were, one might indeed be back in the same unhappy experience again and again. It gives us the exercises of a quickened soul under law who has not yet learned the way of deliverance. This once learned, one is free from the law forever. I have said earlier in the address that primarily here we have a believing Jew struggling to obtain holiness by using the law as a rule of life and resolutely attempting to compel his old nature to be subject to it. In Christendom now the average Gentile believer goes through the same experience; for legality is commonly taught almost everywhere.

Therefore when one is converted it is but natural to reason that now one has been born of God it is only a matter of determination and persistent endeavor to subject oneself to the law, and one will achieve a life of holiness. And God Himself permits the test to be made in order that His people may learn experimentally that the flesh in the believer is no better than the flesh in an unbeliever. When he ceases from self-effort he finds deliverance through the Spirit by occupation with the risen Christ.

Paul writes in the first person singular, not necessarily as depicting a lengthy experience of his own (though he may have gone through it), but in order that each reader may enter into it sympathetically and understandingly for himself.

The law is spiritual, that is, it is of God, it is holy and supernatural. But I am carnal, even though a believer; I am more or less dominated by the flesh. In 1 Cor.2 and 3 we have distinguished for us the natural man, that is, the unsaved man; the carnal man, who is a child of God undelivered; and the spiritual man, the Christian who lives and walks in the Spirit.

Here the carnal man is sold under sin, that is he is subject to the power of the evil nature to which he has died in Christ, a blessed truth indeed, but one which has not yet been apprehended in faith. Consequently he continually finds himself going contrary to the deepest desires of his divinely-implanted new nature. He practises things he does not want to do. He fails to carry out his determinations for good. The sins he commits he hates. The good he loves he has not the strength to perform. But this proves to him that there is a something within him which is to be distinguished from his real self as a child of God. He has the fleshly nature still, though born of God. He knows the law is good. He wants to keep it, and slowly the consciousness dawns upon him that it is not really himself as united to Christ who fails. It is sin, dwelling in him, which is exercising control (vers. 14-17).

So he learns the weakness and unprofitableness of the flesh. "I know," he says, "that in me (that is, in my flesh) dwelleth no good thing." He wants to do good but he lacks the power to perform aright. Still he gives up slowly the effort to force the flesh to behave itself and to be subject to the law.

But the good he would do, he does not, and the evil he would not do, he does. This but establishes him in the conclusion already come to, that, "It is no more I that do it, but sin that dwelleth in me." A law, or principle of action, then, has been discovered. He goes with the good and does the evil. According to the inward man he delights in the law of God, but this does not produce the holiness he expected. He must learn to delight in Christ risen to reach the goal of his desires! This he reaches later, but meantime he is occupied with the discovery of the two natures with their different desires and activities. He detects "another law," a principle, in his members (that is, the members of the body through which the carnal mind works) which wars against the law of his renewed mind taking him captive to the sin-principle which is inseparable from his physical members so long as he is in this life. This principle he calls "the law of sin and death." Were it not for this principle or controlling power there would be no danger of perverting or misusing any human desire, or propensity. Almost convinced that the struggle must go on during the entire course of his earthly existence he cries in anguish, "Oh, wretched man that I am! Who shall deliver me from this body of death!" He is like a living man chained to a polluted, because corrupt, corpse, and unable to snap the chains. He cannot make the corpse clean and subject, no matter how he tries. It is the cry of hopelessness so far as self-effort is concerned. He is brought to the end of human resources. In a moment he gets a vision by faith of the risen Christ. He alone is the Deliverer from Sin's power, as well as the Saviour from the penalty of guilt. "I thank God," he cries, "through Jesus Christ our Lord!" He has found the way out. Not the law but Christ in glory is the rule of life for the Christian.

But the actual entering into this is reserved for the next section. Meantime he confesses "So then with the mind (that is, the renewed mind) I myself (the real man as God sees him) serve the law of God, but with the flesh the law of sin." Such an experience cannot be the Christian ideal. The next chapter which we take up separately shows the way out of this perplexing and unsatisfactory state.

If I am addressing any believer who is even now in the agonizing throes of this terrific struggle, endeavoring to subject the flesh to the holy law of God, let me urge you to accept God's own verdict on the flesh and acknowledge the impossibility of ever making it behave itself. Do not fight with it. It will overthrow you every time. Turn away from it; cease from it altogether; and look away from self and law to Christ risen.

Israel of old wanted to find a short cut through Edom, type of the flesh, but the children of Esau came out armed to contest their way. The command of God was to turn away and "compass the land of Edom." And so with us; it is as we turn altogether from self-occupation we find deliverance and victory in Christ by the Holy Spirit.

LECTURE VI

The Triumph of Grace

PART II

Chapter 8

It has always seemed to me a great pity that in editing our Bibles and dividing the text into chapters and verses the break was permitted to come where it does between chapters seven and eight. I am persuaded that many souls have failed to see the connection just because of this. We get in the habit of reading by chapters, instead of by subjects. Properly, the first four verses of chapter 8 should be joined right on to chapter 7, thus linking with the expression of hope, "I thank God through Jesus Christ our Lord."

These opening verses form a summing up of all the truth previously unfolded in this part of the epistle beginning with chap. 5:12. It is, of course, hardly necessary for me to point out and emphasize what is now familiar to every careful student of the original text: that the last part of verse one is an interpolation (which properly belongs to verse 4), obscuring the sense of the great truth enunciated in the opening words: "There is therefore now no condemnation to those who are in Christ Jesus." This magnificent state, ment requires no qualifying clause. It does not depend on our walk. It is true of all who are in Christ, and to be in Him means to be of the new creation. A glance at the R.V. or any critical translation will show that what I am pointing out is sustained by all the editors. It was man's innate aversion to sovereign grace, I am certain, that brought these qualifying words into the text of the common version. It seemed too much to believe that freedom from condemnation depended on being in Christ Jesus and not upon our walking after the Spirit. So it was easy to lift the words from verse four into verse one. But in verse four they have their proper place for there the question of state is to the fore. In verse one it is the question of standing that is under consideration.

What unspeakable relief it is to the bewildered, troubled soul, oppressed with a sense of his own unworthiness, and distressed because of frequent failures to live up to his own highest resolves, when he learns that God sees him in Christ Jesus, and as thus seen he is free from all condemnation. He may exclaim, "But I *feel* so condemned." This however is not the question. It is not how I feel but it is what God says. He sees me in Christ risen, forever beyond the reach of condemnation.

A prisoner before the bar, hard of hearing and dull of sight, might imagine his doom was being pronounced at the very moment that the judge was giving a verdict of full acquittal. Neither blindness nor deafness would alter this fact. And though we are often slow to hear, and our spiritual vision is most defective, the blessed fact remains that God has pronounced the believer free from condemnation whether he fully rises to the glorious fact or not.

Oh, doubting one, look away then altogether from self and state, look away from frames and feelings to Christ risen, now forever beyond the cross where your sins once put Him, and see yourself in Him, exalted there at God's right hand. He would not be there if the sin question was not settled to the divine satisfaction. The fact that He is there and that you are seen by God in Him is the fullest possible testimony to your freedom from all condemnation.

> "Oh, the peace forever flowing
>   From God's thoughts of His own Son,
> Oh, the peace of simply knowing
>   On the cross that was all done.
>
> Peace with God is Christ in glory,
>   God is light and God is love,
> Jesus died to tell the story,
>   Foes to bring to God above."

We are brought to God "in Christ Jesus," and so all question of judgment is forever settled. It can never be raised again.

This leaves the soul at liberty to be occupied with pleasing God, not as a means of escaping the divine displeasure, but out of love to Him who has brought us to Himself in peace. What the law, with all its stern and solemn warnings and threatenings could not accomplish (that is, produce a life of holiness, because of the weakness and unreliability of the flesh), is now realized in the power of the new life by the Spirit. A clearer reading of verse two would probably be, "The Spirit's law (which is life in Christ Jesus) hath delivered me from the law of sin and death." That is, the Spirit's law of life in Christ Jesus received at new birth is put in contrast to the Law of sin and death against which the believer struggles in vain, as long as he wrestles in his own strength. Victory comes through turning from self to Christ risen. The Spirit's law brings blessing because it gives power to him who had it not before. It is an altogether new principle: life (not in or of ourselves, but) in Christ Jesus. This new life is imparted to the believer, and in the power of this new life he is called to walk. "It is God who worketh in us both the willing and the doing of His good pleasure." The law demanded righteousness from a man whose nature was utterly corrupt and perverted, and which could only bring forth corrupt fruit. The Holy Spirit has produced a new nature in the man in Christ, and linked with this new life are new affections and desires so that he gladly responds to the will of the Lord as revealed in His Word. Thus the righteousness of the law, the good in practice that the law required, is actually produced in the man who walks not after the flesh, not as under the power of the old nature, but after the Spirit, or in subjection to the Spirit, who has come to take possession of us for Christ.

In verses 5 to 27 he proceeds to unfold a wide and soul-uplifting range of truth in connection with the indwelling of the Holy Spirit, who is the only true Vicar of Christ on earth. And first we are reminded that there are two exactly opposite principles to be considered, or two utterly- opposed standards of life. They who are after the flesh, that is, the unsaved, are dominated by the fleshly nature—they "mind the things of the flesh." In these terse words the entire life of the natural man is summed up. In blessed contrast to this they who are after the Spirit, that is those who are born of the Word and the Spirit of God, saved men and women, characteristically mind the things of the Spirit. Parenthetically he explains "the minding of the flesh is death," that is its only legitimate result; but "the minding of the Spirit is life and peace." He who is thus Spirit-controlled is lifted onto a new plain where death has no place and conflict is not known.

It is not that the flesh is, or ever will be, in any sense improved. The flesh in the oldest and godliest Christian is as incorrigibly evil as the flesh in the vilest sinner. "The carnal mind (or, mind of the flesh) is enmity against God: for it is not subject to the law of God, neither indeed can be" (ver. 7). All efforts to reform or purify it are in vain. The law only demonstrates its incurable wickedness. And this explains why the natural man is so utterly unprofitable. "They that are in the flesh cannot please God." It is not of course, that man, as such, does not know right from wrong, or, knowing it, is powerless to do right. To say so would be to declare that man is not a responsible creature but is simply the victim of a hard cruel fatalism. But knowing the evil and approving the good the natural man inclines toward the wrong and fails to do the right, because he is dominated by sin in the flesh, to which he yields his members as instruments of unrighteousness, as we have seen in chapter six, As he is powerless to change his nature he therefore cannot really please God.

But it is otherwise with the believer. He is no longer in the flesh since born of God. He is now in the Spirit, and the Spirit of God dwells in him. "If so be" does not imply that there are Christians who are not indwelt by the Spirit, but has the force of "since," i.e., Since the Spirit of God dwells in you, you are no longer in the flesh;

that is characteristically, as being of the family of the first man, and under the dominion of the old nature. If anyone whether professing to be a believer or not, is devoid of the Spirit of Christ, he is none of His, or "not of Him." It is not merely the disposition of Christ that is in view but the Spirit of Christ is the Holy Spirit whom Christ has sent into the world and who indwells all His redeemed ones in this dispensation of grace. But this, of course, produces a Christ-like disposition in the one so indwelt.

But if Christ (by the Spirit) be thus in us He alone is the source of our power for holiness. We shall get no help from the body. "The body is dead because of sin." It is to be considered as though lifeless and inert so far as ability to produce fruit for God is concerned. All must be of the Spirit. "The Spirit is life because of righteousness."

This is not to ignore or undervalue the body. It too has been purchased by the blood of Christ, and we have the promise that "if the Spirit of Him that raised up Jesus from the dead dwell in you, He that raised up Christ from the dead shall also quicken your mortal bodies by His Spirit that dwelleth in you." (ver. 11.) It is idle to say, as some have done, that this is a present quickening, when the previous verse has told us the very opposite. "The body is dead because of sin"—not actually, of course, but judicially. Therefore we are not to expect anything of it. A strong body does not necessarily mean a strong saint, nor a feeble body a feeble believer. Natural strength may even seem to be a hindrance to spiritual progress if the truth we have been considering be unknown, while feebleness of nature's power may seem to make holiness easier in practice. So monks and ascetics of various kinds have sought to grow in grace by punishing and starving the body. But we are told in Col. 2 that all this is vain and futile so far as checking fleshly indulgence is concerned.

But the body is for the Lord, and the same Holy Spirit who raised up Jesus from the dead will eventually raise us up, by giving resurrection life to these mortal bodies. He is speaking of the body of the living believer who has the new life now, in a body subject to death. It shall put on immortality at the Lord's return. Since God has claimed us for this we owe nothing to the flesh. We are not its debtors to do its service. To do so would only mean to die (it is the great fact to which he calls attention that "sin when it is finished brings forth death"). But, if through the power of the indwelling Spirit we put to death the deeds of the body we shall truly live. The body is viewed as the vehicle through which the flesh acts. It incites the natural appetite to lawless indulgence. The Spirit-led man must be on his guard against this. He has to put to death

these unlawful desires.   In Col. 3:5 we read,
"Mortify therefore your members which are upon
the earth, fornication, uncleanness, inordinate af-
fection, evil concupiscence, and coveteousness
which is idolatry."   Having been crucified with
Christ we are now in faith to mortify by self-
judgment the deeds of the body.   "We which live
are alway delivered unto death for Jesus' sake."

To walk in the flesh is to do contrary to the
whole principle of Christianity, for "as many as
are led (controlled) by the Spirit of God, they are
the sons of God."   It is by this life in the Spirit's
power we mortify the deeds of the body and manifest our new life and relationship.   This is not
a Spirit of bondage, of legality, filling us with fear
and dread, but the Spirit of adoption, of son-ac-
knowledgment, whereby we instinctively lift our
hearts to God in the cry of the conscious child,
"Abba, Father."   Adoption is to be distinguished
from new birth.   We are children by birth but
sons by adoption.   In the full sense we have not
yet received the adoption.   It will all be consum-
mated, as verse 23 shows, at the Lord's return.
When a Roman father publicly acknowledged his
child as his son and heir, legally in the forum,
this ceremony was called "the adoption!"   All
born in his family were children.   Only those
adopted were recognized as sons.   So we have
been born again by the word of God and thus
are children, as were all believers from Abel down.

But as indwelt by the Spirit we are adopted sons, and this will be fully manifested in the most public way when we are changed into our Saviour's image at His coming again.

The child-cry, "Abba, Father," is most suggestive. The one term is Hebrew in the text, the other Greek. For those who are in Christ, the middle wall is broken down. All are one in Him. Together we cry, "Abba, Father." Our Lord Himself used the double term in Gethsemane (see Mark 14:36). Some one has aptly suggested that "Abba" is a word for baby lips, whereas the Greek *pateer,* or the English equivalent, Father, is a word for the more mature. But young and old join together in approaching the Father by the Spirit.

He Himself bears testimony *with* our human spirit that we are God's children. We received His Witness *to* us as given in His Word (Heb. 10: 15) ; thus we have the Witness *in* us, the Word hidden in our hearts (1 Jno.5:10), and now the Spirit Himself takes up His abode within and leads us into the enjoyment of heavenly things. In the text it is "the Spirit itself." The Greek demands this because the word "Spirit" is a neuter noun. But according to English idiom it is correct to use the personal pronoun. He communes with our spirits; He illumines, instructs and guides through the Word.

"Whoso hath felt the Spirit of the Highest,
    Cannot confound, nor doubt Him, nor deny;
Nay, with one voice, O World, though thou
        deniest,
    Stand then on that side, for on this am I."

"The fellowship of the Spirit" is a wonderfully
real thing, known and enjoyed by those who live
and walk in Him.

If children of God it naturally follows that we
are his heirs, and thus we are joint-heirs with
Christ. We share in all His acquired glories, and
so we shall eventually be "glorified together."

In verses 18-27 the apostle contrasts our present state with the coming glory. Even though
thus indwelt by the Spirit we are called to a path
of suffering and sorrow as we follow the steps
of Him who was, on earth, the Man of Sorrows.
But all we can possibly suffer here is as nothing
compared to the glory soon to be manifested.

All creation is expectantly waiting for the full
revelation of the true estate of the sons of God,
when it too shall share in that glorious liberty.
It was made subject to vanity, not of its own will
but through the failure of its federal head, yet
subjected not forever, but in hope of final restoration, and in that day it shall be delivered from
the "bondage of corruption" and made to share
in "the liberty of the glory of the sons of God."

Creation does not share in the liberty of grace. It shall have its part in the liberty of glory, the kingdom age of millennial blessing. Till then the minor note is heard in all creation's sounds; groaning and travailing in birth-pangs through all the present age, waiting for the regeneration; and we ourselves, though we have received the salvation of our souls and have the first-fruits of the Spirit (enjoying a foretaste now of what shall soon be ours in all its fulness), we groan in unison with the groaning creation as we wait expectantly for our acknowledged adoption when we shall receive the redemption of our bodies and be fully like Himself.

In this hope we have been saved and in its power we live. We walk by faith, not by sight. If already seen, hope would fade away, but in this hope we patiently wait for the Lord.

Meantime, often tried to the utmost, we do not know even what we should pray for as we ought, but the indwelling Spirit, knowing the mind of God fully, makes intercession within us according to the will of God, though not in audible words, but with unutterable groanings. "Once we groaned in bondage, now we groan in grace," as another has well said, and this very groaning is in itself a testimony to the changed conditions brought about by our union with Christ. The Spirit's groanings are in harmony with our own sighs and tears, and the great Heart-Searcher hears and answers in wisdom infinite and love unchanging.

And so we go on in peace amid tribulation, assured in our hearts that, "All things work together for good to them who love God, who are the called according to His purpose" (ver. 28). This introduces the closing part of the chapter, and of this great doctrinal division of our epistle, which is a summing up of all we have gone over, and a masterly conclusion to the opening up of "the righteousness of God as revealed in the gospel". It breaks into two sub-sections.

In verses 28 to 34 we have "God for us." In verses 35 to 39, "No separation."

We have a glorious chain of five links in verses 29, 30 reaching from Eternity in the past to Eternity in the future—foreknown, predestinated, called, justified, glorified! Every link was forged in heaven, and not one can ever be broken. This blessed portion is not for theologians to wrangle over but for saints to rejoice in. Foreknown ere we ever trod this globe, we have been predestinated to become fully like our blessed Lord—"conformed to the image of God's Son," that He, who was from all Eternity the "only Begotten," might be "the Firstborn among many brethren." So we have been called by grace divine, justified by faith on the basis of accomplished redemption,

and our glorification is as certain as the foreknow-
ledge of God.

What shall we say to all of this? If God is
thus so manifestly for us—not against us as once
our troubled hearts and guilty consciences made
us believe—what power can be against us? Who
can successfully combat the divine will?

In giving Christ God showed us that (as a
brother beloved has said), "He loved us better
than we loved our sins," and if He did not spare
"His Son but delivered Him up for us all, how
shall He not with Him also freely give us all
things?"

The next two verses should probably all be
thrown into question-form, as in several critical
translations: "Who shall lay anything to the
charge of God's elect? Shall God, who justifieth?
Who shall condemn? Shall Christ who died, yea,
rather, who is risen again, who is even at the
right hand of God, who also maketh intercession
for us?"

There is no answer possible. Every voice is
silenced. Every accusation is hushed. Our standing in Christ is complete and our justification un-
changeable.

And so in the closing verses, 35 to 39, the
apostle triumphantly challenges any possible cir-
cumstance, or personal being in this life or the
next, to attempt to separate the believer from the

love of God which is in Christ Jesus. No experience however hard or difficult can do it. Even though exposed as sheep to the slaughter, yet death but ushers us into the presence of the Lord. In all circumstances we more than conquer, we triumph in Christ.

And so, as he began with this portion with "no condemnation," he ends with "no separation." "I am persuaded that neither death, nor life, nor angels, nor principalities, nor powers, nor things present, nor things to come (and what is there that is neither present nor to come?), nor height, nor depth, nor any other created thing, shall be able to separate us from the love of God which is in Christ Jesus our Lord!"

Blessed, wondrous consummation of the most marvellous theme it was ever given to man to make known to his fellows! May our souls enter ever more deeply into it, and find increasing joy and spiritual strength as we contemplate it.

"No condemnation; blessed is the word!
No separation; forever with the Lord,
By His blood He bought us, cleansed our every
    stain:
With rapture now we'll praise Him.
The Lamb for sinners slain."

—J. DENHAM SMITH.

LECTURES ON ROMANS

LECTURE VII

God's Past Dealings with Israel in Electing Grace

Chapter 9

Having carried us all the way from the distance and bondage and condemnation of chapters 1, 2, and 3 to the glorious freedom and justification and eternal union with Christ of chapter 8, the apostle now turns to consider another phase of things altogether. He well knew that many of his readers would be pious, godly Jews who had accepted Christ as their Messiah and their Saviour, but who were passing through a time of great perplexity and bewilderment as they saw their own nation apparently hardened into opposition against the gospel and sinners of the Gentiles turning to the Lord. They were aware that the prophets predicted a great work of God among the Gentiles, but they had always been ac-

customed to think of this as following upon the
full restoration and blessing of Israel, and, indeed,
as flowing *from* it. Israel should blossom and bud
and fill the face of the whole earth with fruit.
The Gentiles should come to *her* light and find
happiness in subjection to her. Now all the pro-
phecies on which they had based their expecta-
tions seemed to have failed of fulfilment. How
could Paul reconcile his proclamation of free grace
to the Gentiles everywhere, apart from their submission to the rights connected with the old covenant? In the three chapters that are now to occupy us, the apostle meets this question, and that
in a masterly way, showing how the righteousness of God is harmonized with His dispensational
ways. This part of the epistle may be separated
into three sub-divisions. Chapter 9 gives us
God's *past* dealings with Israel in electing grace;
chapter 10, God's *present* dealings with Israel
in governmental discipline; and chapter 11, God's
future dealings with Israel in fulfilment of prophecy.

Opening our Bibles, then, to chapter 9, who can
fail to be touched by his earnest words in regard
to his brethren after the flesh? He insists that
he loves them tenderly, that his heart is constantly burdened because of them. No one could
possibly love them more than he did. They, perhaps, thought him estranged from them because
of his commission to give the gospel to the nations,

but it is very evident, both here and throughout the latter part of the book of Acts, that though he magnified his office as the apostle to the Gentiles, there was always a great tugging at his heart to get to his own people and bear testimony to them. His ministry was ever to the Jew first and then to the Greek.

There is a difference of opinion among men of piety and scholarship as to the exact meaning of verse 3: Did it mean to say that there were times when he had actually wished, if it were possible, to save his brethren by being himself accursed from Christ; that he would have been willing to submit to this? Or is he simply saying that he understands thoroughly the feeling of the most earnest Jew, who in his mistaken zeal detests the Christ, because he himself had at one time actually desired to be accursed from Christ as standing with his brethren after the flesh? If we accept the latter view, we see in this verse simply an expression of the intensity of his feelings as an unconverted Jew. If, as the present lecturer is inclined to do, we accept the former explanation, then we put him on the same platform with Moses, who cried, "If it be possible, blot me out of Thy book, only let the people live." But whichever view we finally accept, our sense of his deep interest in his people becomes intensified as we read.

He enumerates, in verses 4 and 5, the great blessings that belong to Israel. He says that to them pertain the adoption (literally, the son-placing), and the glory, and the covenants, and the giving of the law, and the ritual service, and the promises. "Whose are the fathers, and of whom as concerning the flesh Christ came, who is over all, God blessed forever. Amen."

Consider these blessings in their order:

First: The son-placing. God had owned the nation of Israel as His son. It is not the New Testament truth of individual adoption as we have it in the epistle to the Ephesians and as we have already considered it in Romans 8; in fact, it is not individual here at all, but *national*. God could say of Israel, "Out of Egypt have I called My son;" and, again, "You only have I known of all nations that be upon the earth." They were His, and He owned them as such.

Secondly: The glory. Glory is manifested excellence. And through them God would manifest the excellence of His great name. They were His witnesses.

Third: The covenants. Observe that all the covenants pertain to Israel; that is, the Abrahamic covenant, the Mosaic covenant, the Davidic covenant, and the *new* covenant. All belonged to them. Believers from among the Gentiles come under the blessings of the *new* covenant, because

it is a covenant of pure grace. But God has Israel
and Judah in view when He says, through the
prophet, "I will make a new covenant with you.",
When our Lord instituted the memorial supper,
He said, "This cup is the new covenant in My
blood, which is shed for you for the remission of
sins." The blood of the covenant has already been
poured out, but the new covenant has not yet
actually been made, though it shall be eventually
with the earthly people. Meantime, redeemed
Gentiles come under all the spiritual blessings of
that covenant, and indeed all the others in a
manner far beyond anything that Old Testament
prophets ever could have anticipated.

Fourth: The giving of the law. We have already
seen that the law was given to Israel. It addressed itself to Israel. It was never given to
Gentiles as such, though all men become responsible in regard to its provisions when it is made
known to them.

Fifth: The ritual service. God ordained a ritual
service of marvelous meaning and wondrous
beauty in connection with both the tabernacle and
the temple of old, but there is no hint of ritual-
istic practices of any kind for the Church of God
as such. In fact we are warned against them in
unmistakable terms in Col. 2.

Sixth: The promises. The reference, of course,

is to the many promises of temporal blessing
under Messiah's reign in the kingdom age.

Seventh: The fathers, Abraham, Isaac and
Jacob, the patriarchs, these belonged to the
earthly people.   The heavenly people have no
genealogical list to consult; they are cut off entirely from earthly lineage.   The Church was
chosen in Christ before the foundation of the
world.   But in Israel we see the descendants of
the fathers, though, as the chapter goes on to the
show, they are not all reckoned of Israel who are
of Israel after the flesh.

Of this people Christ came, born of a virgin—
a real man in a true body of flesh and blood with
a rational spirit and soul; nevertheless, as to the
mystery of His person, God over all, blessed forever.

To the faithful Jew who had banked upon the
promises of God to Israel, it would appear that
in large measure these promises had failed; otherwise, why would Israel nationally be set to one
side and the Gentiles be in the place of blessing?
But the apostle now proceeds to show that God
has ever acted on the principle of sovereign
grace.   All the special privileges that Israel had
enjoyed were to be attributed to this principle.
God took them out from among the nations as an
elect people, separating them to Himself.   But He
ever had in mind a *regenerated* people as the people

of the promise. Not all who were born of Israel's
blood belonged to Israel, as recognized by God.
Neither because of the natural seed of Abraham
were they necessarily children of promise. In
electing grace God had said to Abraham, "In
Isaac shall thy seed be called." He chose to pass
over Ishmael, the man born after the flesh, and
take up Isaac, whose birth was miraculous. In
this He illustrates the principle that "they which
are the children of the flesh, these are not the
children of God. Children of promise are counted
for the seed." What a staggering blow is this to
the pretensions of those who boast so loudly in
our day of what they call the *universal fatherhood
of God and brotherhood of man.* The children of the
flesh, we are distinctly told, are *not* the children
of God. And in this statement we have, empha-
sized, the same truth that our Lord declared to
Nicodemus, "Except a man be born again, he cannot see the kingdom of God."

Isaac was the child of promise. God said, "At
this time will I come, and Sarah shall have a
son." Naturally, it would have been impossible
for the promise to be fulfilled, but God wrought
in resurrection power, quickening the dead bodies
of Isaac's parents, and the word came true.

Then again, in the case of the children of Isaac
and Rebecca, we see the same principle of electing grace illustrated. We are told that:

"(For the children being not yet born, neither having done any good or evil, that the purpose of God according to election might stand, not of works, but of Him that calleth;) It was said unto her, The elder shall serve the younger. As it is written, Jacob have I loved, but Esau have I hated" (vers. 11-13).

What a tremendous amount of needless controversy has raged about these verses! Yet how plain and simple they are, viewed in the light of God's dispensational dealings. There is no question here of predestination to heaven or reprobation to hell; in fact, eternal issues do not really come in throughout this chapter, although, of course, they naturally follow as the result of the use or abuse of God-given privileges. But we are not told here, nor anywhere else, that before children are born it is God's purpose to send one to heaven and another to hell; to save one by grace, notwithstanding all his evil works, and to condemn the other to perdition, notwithstanding all his yearnings for something higher and nobler than he has yet found The passage has to do entirely with privilege here on earth. It was the purpose of God that Jacob should be the father of the nation of Israel, and that *through* him the promised Seed, our Lord Jesus Christ, should come into the world. He had also pre-determined that Esau should be a man of the wilderness— the father of a nation of nomads, as the Edomites

have ever been. It is this that is involved in the
pre-natal decree: "The elder shall serve the
younger." And be it observed that it was not
before the children were born, neither had done
any good or evil, that God said, "Jacob have I
loved, but Esau have I hated." These words are
quoted from the very last book of the Old Testament. We find them in Malachi 1: 2, 3. Let me
read them:

"I have loved you, saith the Lord, yet ye say,
Wherein hast thou loved us? Was not Esau
Jacob's brother? saith the Lord: yet I loved
Jacob, and I hated Esau, and laid his mountains
and his heritage waste for the dragons of the
wilderness."

Observe what is in question:—God is plead-
ing with the sons of Jacob to serve and obey Him,
on the ground that He is doubly entitled to their
obedience, first, because He is their Creator,
second, because of the privileges, the earthly
blessings He has given them. Comparatively
speaking, He has loved Jacob, and hated Esau.
That is, He gave to Jacob a beautiful fatherland,
well-watered, productive, delightful for situation;
He gave them, too, a holy law, pastors, shepherd-
kings to guide them, prophets to instruct them,
a ritual system full and expressive to lead their
hearts out in worship and praise. All these things
were denied to Edom. They were the children

of the desert. We do not read that a prophet
was ever sent to them, though they were not left
without some knowledge of God. Esau received
instruction from the lips of his parents, but for
a morsel of bread he sold his birthright. And
his descendants have ever been characterized by
the same independent lawless spirit. Dispensa-
tionally, Jacob was loved, Esau hated. There is
no reference to the individual as such. "God
so loved the world," and therefore every child
of Jacob or of Esau may be saved who will. But
no one can dispute the fact that Jacob and his
descendants enjoyed earthly privileges, and spiritual, too, that Esau and his children had never
known. Is God unrighteous in thus distinguish-
ing between nations? Is He unrighteous, for instance, to-day in giving to the peoples of northern
Europe and of America privileges that the inhabi-
tants of central Africa and inland South America
have never known? By no means. He is
sovereign. He distributes the nations of men
upon the earth as seems good to Himself, and
though He takes up one nation in special grace
and passes by another, that does not in the
slightest degree hinder any individual in any
nation from turning to God in repentance, and if
any men anywhere under the sun, in any circumstances whatever, look up to God, no matter how
deep their ignorance, confessing their sin and
crying out for mercy, it is written, "Whosoever

shall call upon the name of the Lord shall be saved."

Paul quotes the word of God to Moses: "I will have mercy on whom I *will* have mercy, and I will have compassion on whom I *will* have compassion."

Observe, you do not get the negative. He does not say, "I will condemn whom I will condemn, or I will reprobate to eternal destruction whom I will reprobate." There is no such thought in the mind of God, who "desireth not the death of the sinner, but that all should turn to Him and live." When were these words spoken to Moses? Turn back to Exodus 33:19. Read the entire passage, and note the occasion on which God used them. Israel had forfeited all claim to blessing on the ground of law; they had made a calf of gold and bowed down before it, even while Moses was in the mount receiving the tables of the covenant. Thus they had violated the first two commandments before they were brought into the camp, after having declared but a few days before, "All that the Lord hath spoken will we do, and be obedient." *Because* of this, God was about to blot them out from the face of the earth, but Moses, the mediator, pleaded their cause in His presence. He even offered, as we have seen, to die in their stead, if that might turn aside the fierce anger of the Lord. But now observe the wonders of sovereign grace: God took refuge in His own inherent right to suspend judgment, if it pleased Him. And so He exclaims, "I will be gracious to whom I *will* be gracious, and I will show mercy on whom I *will* show mercy." He spared the people, thus making them a wondrous witness to His grace. Apart from this sovereign grace no one would ever be saved, because *all* men have forfeited title to life through sin. Israel, nationally, owed all their blessing to God's mercy and compassion, when in righteousness they would have been cut off from the land of the living. If it pleased God now to take up the Gentiles and show mercy to them, what ground had Israel to complain?

So, then, exclaims the apostle, "It is not of him that willeth, nor of him that runneth, but of God that showeth mercy." He is not setting aside the will of man; he is not declaring that no responsibility to run in the way of righteousness rests upon man; but he *is* declaring that, apart from the sovereign mercy of God, no man would ever will to be saved or run in the way of His commandments.

He turns next to speak of Pharaoh, for it is evident that one cannot logically accept the truth already demonstrated without recognizing the fact that God *does* give some up to destruction and leave them to perish in their sins. Pharaoh was a Gentile, the oppressor of Israel. To him God sent His servants demanding submission. In his pride and haughtiness, in his brazenness and

wickedness, he exclaimed, "Who is the Lord, that
I should obey Him?" He dares to challenge
the Almighty, and God condescends to accept the
challenge. He says:

"Even for this same purpose have I raised thee
up, that I might show My power in thee, and
that My name might be declared throughout
all the earth."

He is not speaking here of a helpless babe. The
words have no reference to the birth of Pharaoh;
they have to do exclusively with the outstanding
position that God gave him in order that he might
be a lesson to all succeeding generations of the
folly of fighting against God. The Greeks used
to say, "Whom the gods would destroy, they first
make mad." It was a principle that even the
heathen could plainly discern. We see the same
principle still: an Alexander, a Caesar, a Napoleon,
a Kaiser permitted to climb to the very summit,
almost, of human ambition, only to be hurled
ignominiously into the depths of execration at
last.

And so God demonstrates that He hath mercy
on whom He *will* have mercy, and whom He will,
He hardeneth. He is the moral governor of the
universe and He worketh all things according to
the counsel of His own will. "None can stay His
hand, nor say unto God, What doest Thou?" If
men dare to rush ruthlessly upon the thick bosses

of the Almighty they must experience His righteous wrath.

Beginning with verse 19, and going on to the end of the chapter, the apostle undertakes to meet the objection of the fatalist, the man who says, "Well, granting all you've been saying, then God's decrees are irresistible and I myself am but an automaton, moved about at His will, absolutely without responsibility. Why does He find fault? What ground can there be for judgment of a creature who can never will nor run but as God Himself directs? To resist His will is impossible. Where, then, does moral responsibility come in?"

Such objections to the doctrine of the Divine Sovereignty have been raised from the earliest days. But, inasmuch as we have already seen that the apostle simply has in view privilege here on earth, those objections fall to the ground. The privileged Jew may fail utterly to appreciate the blessings lavished upon him, and so come under divine condemnation; while the ignorant barbarian, bereft of all the blessings of civilization and enlightenment, may, nevertheless, have an exercised conscience that will lead him into the presence of God. At any rate, it is the height of impiety for puny man to sit in judgment upon God. It is as though the vessel wrought upon the wheel should turn to the potter and ask, indignantly, "Why hast thou made me thus?" Clearly, he who has the intelligence to form vessels out of

clay has the right to make them of such shape
or size or for such use as he deems best. Of the
very same lump of clay he may make one vessel
unto honor, to be displayed upon the sideboard to
admiring throngs, and another unto dishonor,
for use in a scullery, and altogether without
beauty or attractiveness. If God, the great
Former of all, willing to manifest both His anger
and His power, endures, with much long-suffering, vessels that call down His indignation because
having a will, which the work of the potter has
not, they deliberately fit themselves for destruction, shall anyone find fault if He manifests the
riches of His glory in His dealings with other
vessels of mercy which He has had in view for
the glory of His Son from eternity? And such
vessels of mercy are the called of God, whether
Jews by birth or Gentiles also. Passage after passage from the Old Testament is called into requi-
sition to show that this is nothing new in God's
ways with men, and that the prophets have foreseen just such a setting aside of Israel and taking
up of the Gentiles as has already taken place.
Hosea testified that God has said, "I will call them
My people which were not My people, and her beloved which was not beloved. And it shall come
to pass that in the place where it was said
unto them, 'Ye are not My people', they shall be
called the children of the living God." Israel
forfeited all title to be called His people. During

the present dispensation, when grace is going out
to the Gentiles, they would be set to one side
nationally, as by-and-by the same grace that is now
being shown to the nations will be manifested
again to them, and they shall once more be called
the children of the living God. Isaiah prophesied
that although the number of the children of Israel
should be as the sands of the sea, yet of this vast
throng only a remnant should be saved, and that
in the day of the Lord's indignation, when He
would be executing His judgment upon the earth.
The same prophet saw the sin of the people as the
sin of the cities of the plain, and exclaimed,
"Except the Lord of hosts hath left us a seed, we
should be as Sodom, and be made like unto Go-
morrah."

What then, is the conclusion? Simply that the
unrighteous Gentiles have, through grace, at-
tained to a righteousness which is of faith. They
followed not after righteousness, but God in righteousness pursued after them and made known His
gospel, that they might believe and be saved.
Israel, on the other hand, to whom He had given
a law of righteousness, were even more guilty
than the Gentiles, for they refused to follow it
and therefore they missed that righteousness
which the law would have inculcated.

Why did they miss it? Because they failed to
realize that is it only to be obtained by faith, and
that no man, by his own power, can ever keep that

holy and perfect law. When God sent His Son
into the world, who is the embodiment of all perfection, in whom the law was fulfilled perfectly,
they knew Him not, but stumbled over the stumbling stone of a lowly Christ when they were expect-
ing a triumphant King.   They realized not their
need of one who could accomplish righteousness
on their behalf, because they lacked faith. And
so they fulfilled the Scripture in condemning Him.
But, nevertheless, wherever He is individually received by faith, He saves the soul that trusts
Him, though the nation has stumbled and fallen.
According as it is written, "Behold, I lay in Zion a
stumbling stone, and a rock of offence, and whosoever believeth on Him shall not be ashamed."
When He came in grace the first time, Israel refused Him.   But "the stone that the builders rejected is made the Head of the corner."   When
He comes again He will be as the stone, falling in
judgment upon the Gentiles, whereas Israel then
repentant and regenerated will see in Him the
chief corner stone.

God's Present Dealings with Israel in Governmental Discipline

Chapter 10

Having, as we have seen, vindicated in a masterly way the righteousness of God in setting aside Israel nationally because of unbelief, and taking up the Gentiles during the present dispensation of grace, the apostle now goes on to show that this deflection of the nation as such does not in any wise involve the rejection of the individual Israelite. The nation as such is no longer looked upon as in covenant relationship with God, nor will it be until it comes under the new covenant at the beginning of the millennium; when "a nation shall be born in a day;" but the same promises apply to any individual member of the house of Israel as to any individual Gentile.

In the first three verses the apostle expresses his yearning desire and prayer for his kinsmen. He longs and prays that they may be saved, for though Abraham's seed after the flesh, they are "lost sheep," and need to be sought and found by the Good Shepherd just as truly as those "other sheep" of the Gentiles. But the pitiable thing

is that, although lost, they do not realize their true
condition. Filled with a mistaken zeal for God,
marked by an outward adherence to Judaism as
a divinely-established system, they are earnestly
trying to serve the God of their fathers, but not
according to knowledge; that is, they have refused
the fuller revelation He has given of Himself,
His mind, and His will through Christ Jesus.
"For they being ignorant of God's righteousness
and going about to establish their own righteousness, have not submitted themselves unto the
righteousness of God."

The term "God's righteousness" is used here
somewhat differently to the general expression,
the "righteousness of God." We have seen here-
tofore that the righteousness of God is used in
two ways: It is God's consistency with Himself,
as one has expressed it, and thereby becomes the
great sheet-anchor of the soul, because in the gospel God has revealed how He can be just and the
Justifier of those who put faith in Christ; the
sin question has been settled in a righteous way,
as God's nature demanded that it should be, ere
He could deal in grace with guilty men. The
second aspect is that of imputation. God imputes
righteousness to all who believe. Therefore
Christ, and Christ Himself, is the righteousness of
the believer. We are thus made, or constituted,
the righteousness of God in Him according as
it is written in the book of the prophet Jeremiah:

"This is His name whereby He shall be called, The Lord our Righteousness" (Jehovah Tsidkenu).

But in these three verses where the apostle says, "They being ignorant of God's righteousness," it seems plain that he simply means that they are ignorant of how righteous God really is; therefore they go about attempting to establish a righteousness of their own. No man would think of doing this, if he realized for a moment the transcendent character of the divine righteousness. The utter impossibility of producing a righteousness of works suitable for a God of such infinite righteousness would cause the soul to shrink back in acknowledgement of his own helplessness. It is when men reach this place that they are ready to submit themselves unto that righteousness of God which has been revealed in the gospel. When I learn that I am absolutely without righteousness in myself; that is, without such a righteousness as is suited to a righteous God, then I am glad to avail myself of that righteousness which He Himself proclaims in the gospel, and in which He clothes me when I trust in Christ. "For Christ is the end (i.e., the object for the consummation) of the law for righteousness to every one that believeth." The law proposed a righteousness which I could not furnish. Christ has met every requirement of that holy law, He has died under its penalty; He has risen from the dead; He is Himself the righteousness which all need.

In the verses that follow, the apostle contrasts *legal* righteousness or a "by works righteousness" with this "in *faith* righteousness." He cites from Moses, who describes legal righteousness in the solemn words, "The man which doeth those things shall live by them" (See Lev. 18:5). This is law in its very essence, "Do and live." But no man ever yet *did* that which entitled him to life, for "if a man should keep the whole law and yet offend in one point, he is guilty of all"; that is, he is a law-breaker. He has not necessarily violated every commandment. But a thief is as truly a law-breaker as a murderer. And the law having been violated, even once, man's title to life thereunder is forfeited.

Now the righteousness which is of faith depends upon testimony that God has given. Again the apostle quotes from Moses, who, in Deuteronomy 30:12-14, presses upon the people the fact that God has given testimony which man is responsible to believe. The testimony there, of course, was the revelation from Sinai. But the apostle takes up Moses' words, and in a wonderful way under the guidance of the Spirit, applies them to Christ. "Say not in thine heart, Who shall ascend into heaven? (that is, to bring Christ down from above:) Or, Who shall descend into the deep? (that is, to bring up Christ again from the dead.)" Christ has already come down. He has died. God has raised Him from the dead. And upon this depends the entire gospel testimony.

Therefore he goes on to say, "The word is nigh thee, even in thy mouth, and in thy heart: that is, the word of faith, which we preach." The gospel has been proclaimed; they have heard it; they are familiar with its terms. The question is: Do they believe it and confess the Christ it proclaims as their Lord? For in verses 9 and 10 he epitomises the whole matter in words that have been used of God through the centuries to bring assurance to thousands of precious souls, "That if thou shalt confess with thy mouth the Lord Jesus" (or literally, Jesus as Lord), "and shalt believe in thine heart that God hath raised Him from the dead, thou shalt be saved. For with the heart man believeth unto righteousness; and with the mouth confession is made unto salvation." The heart is simply another term for the real man. The apostle is not trying to draw a fine distinction, as some preachers do, between believing with the head and believing with the heart. He does not occupy us with the *nature* of belief; he *does* occupy us with the *object* of faith. We believe the message that God has given concerning Christ. If we believe at all, we believe with the heart. Otherwise we do not really trust. "With the heart" man believeth. The confession

here is not, of course, necessarily the same thing
as where our Lord says, "Whosoever shall confess
Me before men, him will I confess before My
Father which is in heaven." This is rather the
soul's confession to God Himself that he takes
Jesus as Lord.

He then cites another Old Testament scripture
from the book of the prophet Isaiah (ch.28:16),
which declares that "Whosoever believeth on Him
shall not be ashamed." In this way he proves
that the universality of the present gospel faith
is in no wise in conflict with the revealed word
of God as given to the Jew of old. "Whosoever"
includes the whole world. Already he has established the fact in Chapter 3 that there is no
difference between Jew and Gentile, so far as sin
is concerned. Now he gives the other side of the
"no difference" doctrine. "The same Lord over all is
rich unto all that call upon Him, for whosoever
shall call upon the name of the Lord shall be
saved." To *call* upon the name of the Lord is, of
course, to invoke His name in faith. His name
speaks of what He is. He who calls upon the name
of the Lord puts his trust in Him, as it is written,
"The name of the Lord is a strong tower, and the
righteous runneth into it and is safe."

The Jew had been accustomed to think of himself as the chosen of the Lord, and as the one to
whom was committed the testimony of the one
true and living God. Therefore the objector

naturally asks, and Paul puts the very words in
his mouth, "How then shall they call on Him in
whom they have not believed?" And he follows
this question with another: "And how shall they
believe in Him of whom they have not heard?"
And this again with a third question: "How shall
they hear without a preacher?" Nor are the
objections ended with this, for again he says:
"And how shall they preach, except they be sent?
As it is written, How beautiful are the feet of
them that preach the gospel of peace, and bring
glad tidings of good things!" The Jew believed
in God; he had heard of Him; to him preachers
had proclaimed the message, and these preachers
had been sent of God. But who authorized anyone to overleap the Jewish bounds and go with
the gospel of peace to the Gentiles?

In reply to the objector, Paul reminds him that
Israel who had all these privileges had not re-
sponded as might have been expected; not all had
obeyed the gospel. And this, too, was foreseen
by the Old Testament prophets. Isaiah sadly
asked, "Lord, who hath believed our report?"
indicating that many who heard would refuse to
accept this message. But then the objector
answers, "You admit, Paul, that faith comes by
hearing, and hearing by the Word, or the report
of God." "Yes," he replies, "but have they not
heard? Is there any people so utterly dark and
ignorant that the word of God in some form has

not come to them, thus putting them into responsibility?" Psalm 19 testifies that the voice of
God may be heard in His creation: the sun, the
moon, the stars—all the marvels of this wonderful universe—testify to the reality of a *personal*
Creator. And so the Psalmist says, "Their sound
went unto all the earth, and their words unto the
end of the world."

It is not a new thing, then, for God to speak to
Gentiles. All that is new about it is that He is
now speaking more fully, more clearly than He
ever spoke before. He is now proclaiming in unmistakable terms an offer of salvation to all who
trust His word. And did not Israel know that God
was going to take up the peoples of the nations?
They *should* have known, for Moses himself said:
"I will provoke you to jealousy by them that are
no people, and by a foolish nation I will anger
you." And Isaiah, with uncompromising boldness,
declares: "I was found of them that sought Me
not; I was made manifest unto them that asked
not after Me." Surely words like these could
only apply to the heathen of the Gentile world.
And as for Israel, with all their privileges, concerning them God had said: "All day long I have
stretched forth My hands unto a disobedient and
gainsaying people." The subject is continued in
the opening verses of the next chapter, in which,
as we shall see, the apostle shows how God is
getting His election, even out of Israel, during

the present dispensation. But we will consider the entire chapter in one address, and so I forbear further comment now, save to insist that the gist of the present portion is evidently this: during the present dispensation, when grace is going out to the nations, beyond the bounds of the Jewish race, this does not involve the utter rejection of Israelites, but it does imply the end of special privilege. They may be saved if they will, but on exactly the same terms as the despised Gentile. The middle wall of partition is broken down, but grace is offered through Jesus Christ to all who own their guilt and confess His name.

LECTURE IX

God's Future Dealings with Israel in Fulfilment of the Prophetic Scriptures

Chapter 11

This eleventh chapter is most illuminating in regard to God's dispensational plan. We have already seen how His past dealings with Israel proved His righteousness in acting toward the Gentiles as He now does, despite the covenant made with the earthly people. Then in chapter 10 we have seen that although the nation as such is set to one side, this does not in any way hinder the individual Israelite from turning to God and finding that same salvation which He, in His sovereignty, is proclaiming through His servants to the Gentiles. In the first part of our present chapter, verses 1 to 6, the subject of chapter 10 is continued and brought to a conclusion. The question is asked: "Hath God cast away His people?" By no means. Paul's own experiences proved that this was not the case; for he was an Israelite, of the natural seed of Abraham, and of the tribe of Benjamin; yet he had been laid hold of by the Spirit of God and brought to a saving knowledge of the Lord Jesus Christ. And

what was true of him *might* be true of any other.
What had really happened was simply the fulfilment of the words of the prophet Elijah in
a wider sense than when he spoke in Ahab's day.
The nation had rejected every testimony sent to it.
As a people they had killed the prophets and de-
filed Jehovah's altar.   But as in Elijah's day, God
had reserved seven thousand to Himself who had
not bowed the knee to the image of Baal, so "at
this present time also there is a remnant according to the election of grace."   God rejects the
nation, but grace goes out to the individual.

The great thing, however, for Israel to understand is that, if saved at all, they are saved
exactly as Gentiles are saved, and that is by grace.
Grace, as we have seen, is unmerited favor.   Yea,
we may put it even stronger: it is favor against
merit.   This precludes all thought of work.   If
merit of any sort is taken into consideration, then
it is no more grace.   On the other hand, if salvation be of works, this leaves no place whatever for
grace, because it would take from work its merit-
orious character.   The two principles—salvation
by grace and salvation by works—are diametri-
cally opposed, one to the other.   There can be no
admixture of law and grace; they are mutually
destructive principles.

Beginning with verse 7, the apostle now undertakes to show God's secret purpose in connection

with Israel in the coming day. What the nation sought it has failed to obtain; but the election (that is, those who are content to be saved by grace) *do* obtain it; and as to the rest, they are judicially blinded. Again he quotes from the Old Testament to show that this is in full accord with the prophetic Word. As Isaiah wrote, "God hath given them the spirit of slumber, eyes that they should not see, and ears that they should not hear;" and He shows that this is true unto this day. David, too, had written: "Let their table be made a snare, and a trap, and a stumbling-block, and a recompense unto them: let their eyes be darkened, that they may not see, and bow down their back alway." These terrible imprecations were fulfilled when the representatives of the nation deliberately rejected Christ and called down judgment upon the heads of their descendants when they cried in Pilate's judgment hall, "His blood be upon us, and upon our children." Rejecting Messiah, God rejected them. And many Christians have taken it for granted that He is through with them as a nation forever. This, the apostle now shows, is far from the truth. He asks, "Have they stumbled that they should fall?"; that is, utterly fall, fall without any hope or possibility of recovering. The answer again is, "By no means." God has overruled their present defection to make known His riches of grace toward the Gentiles, and this, in turn, will be used

eventually to provoke Israel to jealousy and to turn
them back to the God of their fathers and to the
Christ whom they have rejected. This recovery
will be a means of untold blessing to that part
of the world which has not yet come to a saving
knowledge of the gospel. With holy enthusiasm
he exclaims: "Now if the defection of them be
the riches of the world, and the diminishing of
them the riches of the Gentiles; how much more
their fulness?" It is well to note the use he
makes of this word, "fulness," as we shall come
upon it lower down in the chapter. The fulness
of Israel will be the conversion of Israel—the fulfilment of God's purpose regarding them.

Paul was the apostle to the Gentiles, and as
such, he magnified his office; but he would not
have the Gentiles for a moment think that he had
lost his interest in Israel: rather he would see
them stirred to emulation, that many might be
saved from among them as they saw the grace of
God going out to the Gentiles; on the other hand,
he would not have the Gentile glory over the
Jew because the latter was set aside and the
former enjoyed the blessings that the Jew would
have had, had he been ready to receive them. He
continues his argument by introducing a parable,
which brings out most vividly the divine plan.
He says: "For if the casting away of them be the
reconciling of the world, what shall the receiving
of them be, but life from the dead?" That is, if,

as they wander among all the nations, a disappointed and weary people, under the ban of the God of their fathers, the message of grace is going out to the Gentiles, and an election from them are receiving the message, what will it mean to the world as a whole when Israel *nationally* will turn back to the Lord and become in very truth a holy people, His witnesses to all nations?

"For if the firstfruit be holy, the lump is also holy: and if the root be holy, so are the branches." If the regenerated remnant in Israel be indeed a people set apart to God, so eventually will the nation be to which they belong. And if the root of the covenant olive tree be holy (that is, Abraham, who believed God, and it was counted to him for righteousness), so are all those who are really linked with him by faith. They were *natural* branches in the olive tree—Israelites by birth but not by grace, who were broken off. And in order that the promises of God to Abraham should not fail, "In thy seed shall all the nations of the earth be blessed," the branches of the wild olive tree—the Gentiles—were grafted in among the remnant of Israel, and thus Jew and Gentile believing together, partake of the root and fatness of the olive tree. But now the grave danger is lest the Gentile should rest on mere outward privileges, and while linked with the children of the promise, should fail to appreciate for themselves the gospel of God, and so prove unreal. In that case, God will have to deal with the Gentiles as He had dealt with the Jews. And so we get the solemn warning: "Boast not against the branches. But if thou boast, thou bearest not the root, but the root thee." Some might say, "Well, but the natural branches were broken off, that I, a Gentile, might be grafted in." The answer is clear and distinct: "They were broken off because of unbelief, and thou standest by faith." Therefore the admonition, "Be not high-minded, but fear: for if God spared not the natural branches, take heed lest He also spare not thee."

Do we need to pause to ask whether the Gentiles have valued their privileges? Is it not patent to every observing spiritually-minded person that conditions in Christendom are as bad to-day as they ever were in Israel? Do we not see apostasy from the truth everywhere prevalent? Are not the characteristic features of the last days, as depicted in 2nd Timothy 3, everywhere manifest? If so, may we not well be warned that the time is near when the unfruitful branches will be torn out of the olive tree and the natural branches, at last turning back to God, be grafted in again to their own olive tree?

In these dispensational ways we see manifested that goodness and severity of God, which has already been so clearly brought out in the ninth chapter: on those who fell, who refused to believe the testimony, severity; but toward ignorant and unworthy Gentiles, goodness, but this goodness only to be continued toward them if they continue to appreciate it, otherwise they, too, shall be cut off. Who can doubt that the day of the cutting off is near at hand, when the true Church having been caught up to be with the Lord, judgment will be meted out to unfaithful Christendom, and then God will turn back in grace to Israel, if they abide not still in unbelief, and they shall be re-grafted into their own olive tree, according to the power of the God of resurrection?

I recall an article by a well-known "higher critic," which I read some years ago, in which he was ridiculing the idea of the apostle Paul's inspiration because of his apparent ignorance of one of the first principles of horticulture: "Paul," said he, "was actually so ignorant of the art of grafting that he speaks of grafting wild branches into a good tree, evidently not aware of the fact that it is customary to graft good branches into a wild tree." It is clear that the reverend critic had never carefully read the apostle's own words, as given in the next verse, or he would not have been caught in such a trap. Paul clearly indicates that his illustration is one which he well knew to be opposed to that which was ordinarily done. He says: "For if thou wert cut out of the olive tree which is wild by nature, and wert graffed *contrary* to nature into a good olive tree: how much more shall these, which be the natural branches, be graffed into their own olive tree?"

No; Paul was not ignorant of horticulture, nor was the Holy Ghost ignorant, who was guiding him and inspiring him as he wrote. That which is not customary to man is often in full accord with the divine plan, as here.

And so, in verses 25-32, we see just what must take place before this re-grafting, and what will follow afterwards. "I would not, brethren, that ye should be ignorant of this mystery, lest ye should be wise in your own conceits; that blindness in part has happened to Israel, until the fulness of the Gentiles be come in. And so all Israel shall be saved."

This, then, is one of the secret things hidden in the mind of God until the due time for its revelation: Israel will be blinded in part, but, thank God, only in part, until the present work of God among the Gentiles be completed. Here we have the second use of this word "fulness." "The fulness of the Gentiles" is the completion of the work among the nations which has been going on ever since Israel's rejection. This "fulness," as we know from other scriptures, will come in when our Lord calls His Church to be with Himself, in accordance with 1 Thessalonians 4, and 1 Corinthians 15. It is then that "all Israel shall be saved." We are not to understand by the term "all Israel" everyone of Israel's blood, for we have already learned that "they are not all Israel who are of Israel, but the children of the promise are counted for the seed." So the remnant will be the true Israel in that glorious day when, "There shall come out of the Zion the Deliverer, and shall turn away ungodliness from Jacob," for God has said: "This is My covenant unto them when I shall take away their sins."

So then, the apostle concludes, they are enemies of the gospel for the present time; but through their enmity grace goes out to the Gentiles. Nevertheless, according to the divine plan, they are still beloved for the fathers' sakes, for God's gifts and calling He never retracts; the promises made to the patriarchs and to David shall and *must* be fulfilled. Study carefully psalm 89 in this connection. And just as the Gentiles, who in time past had not believed God but have now obtained mercy through the Jews' unbelief, so, in like manner, when the Gentiles prove unbelieving and are set to one side, Israel will obtain mercy when they turn back in faith to God.

Whether Jew or Gentile, all alike are saved on the same principle, "For God hath concluded all in unbelief, that He might have mercy upon all."

The last four verses are in the nature of a Doxology. The apostle's heart is filled with worship, and praise, and admiration as the full blaze of the divine plan fills the horizon of his soul. He exclaims: "O the depths of the riches both of the wisdom and knowledge of God! How unsearchable are His judgments, and His ways past finding out!"

Apart from revelation none could have known His mind, just as no created being could ever have been His counsellor. No one ever earned grace by first giving to Him, in order that blessing might be recompensed; but everything is *of* Him, and *through* Him, and *unto* Him, to whom be glory forever. Amen.

LECTURES ON ROMANS

DIVISION III.   PRACTICAL.

Divine Righteousness Producing Practical Righteousness
in the Believer

Chapters 12-16

LECTURE X

The Walk of the Christian in Relation to his Fellow-Believers, and to Men of the World

Chapter 12

We come now to consider the practical bearing
of all this precious truth, which the Spirit of
God has been unfolding before our astonished
eyes.   In this last part of the epistle we learn
what the effect should be upon the believer who
has laid hold, by faith, of the truth of the gospel.
We may divide this third part, roughly, as follows:
Sub-division 1, Chapters 12:1—15:7, God's good
and acceptable and perfect will unfolded; Subdivision 2, Chapter 15:8-33, which divides into
two parts the conclusion of the matter and his
own service; Sub-division 3, Chapter 16:1-24,
Salutations and Warning.   Verses 25-27 form an
appendix to the entire epistle.

The first two verses of Chapter 12 are the introduction to this entire practical part of the letter, based upon the revelation given in Chapters 1-8, for we may very properly consider Chapters 9-11 as a great parenthesis, occasioned because of the necessity of clearing the mind of the believing Jew in regard to the ways of God.

The opening words necessarily link with the closing part of Chapter 8: "I beseech you, therefore, brethren." The "therefore" refers clearly to the magnificent summing up of Christian standing and eternal blessing in the eighth chapter. Because you are in Christ free from all condemnation; because you are indwelt by the Holy Spirit; because you are sons by adoption, because you are eternally linked up with Christ; because you are the elect of God, predestined to be conformed to the image of His Son; because you are beyond all possibility of condemnation, since Christ has died and been raised again and sits at God's right hand; because no charge can ever be laid against the believer that God will hear; because there is no separation from the love of God for those who are in Christ Jesus—"I beseech you to present your bodies a living sacrifice, holy, acceptable unto God, which is your intelligent service!" Christ gave Himself for us—a sacrifice in death. Like the first-born in Egypt, redeemed by the blood of the lamb, you are now to be devoted to Him. As the Levites were afterwards

presented to God to live sacrificial lives in place of
the first-born, so each believer is called upon to
recognize the Lord's claims upon him, and to present, or yield, his body as a living sacrifice, set
apart and acceptable unto God, because of the
price that has been paid for his redemption. See
Num. 8:11-21, and Daniel 3:28. How much do we
really know of this experimentally? We who once
yielded our members to the service of sin and
Satan, are now called upon to yield ourselves
wholly unto God as those who are alive from the
dead. This will involve sacrifice all the way, the
denial of self, and the constant recognition of the
divine claims upon us.

The second verse makes clearer the meaning
involved: "Be not conformed to this world: but
be ye transformed by the renewing of your mind,
that ye may prove what is that good, and acceptable, and perfect, will of God."

The cross of Christ has come in between the
believer and the world. To conform himself to the
ways of this present evil age is to be unfaithful
to the One whom the world has rejected but whom
we have owned as Lord and Saviour. "I would
give the world to have your experience," said a
young woman on one occasion to a devoted Christian lady. "My dear," was the reply, "that's
exactly what it cost me. I gave the world for it."
The loyal heart exclaims with gladness, not grudg-
ingly,

> "Take the world, but give me Jesus;
>   All earth's joys are but in name;
> But His love abideth ever,
>   Through eternal years the same."

Moved by the "expulsive power of a new affec-
tion," it becomes easy for the soul to say with
Paul: "God forbid that I should glory, save in the
cross of the Lord Jesus Christ, by which the
world is crucified unto me and I unto the world."

We are not to suppose that non-conformity to
the world necessarily involves awkwardness of
behavior, peculiarity of dress, or boorishness in
manner.   But the entire world system is summed
up in three terms: the lust of the flesh, the
lust of the eye and the pride of life, or the osten-
tation of living.   Therefore non-conformity to
the world implies holding the body and its appe-
tites in subjection to the Spirit of God, subject-
ing the imagination to the mind of Christ, and
walking in lowliness of spirit through a scene
where self-confidence and boasting are the order
of the day.

In 2 Corinthians 3 we read that, "We all, be-
holding as in a glass, the glory of the unveiled
face of the Lord, are changed (or transformed)
into the same image by the Spirit of the Lord"
(literal rendering).

And so here we are commanded to be transformed by the renewing of our minds; that is,

as the mind is occupied with Christ and the affections set on things above, we become like Him who has won our hearts for Himself; and walking in loving obedience, we prove the blessedness of the good, and acceptable, and perfect, will of God. Through the rest of the chapter we have God's good will in regard to our relations, particularly to fellow-believers; in chapter 13, the will of God for the believer in relation to human government and society in general; in chapter 14 and the first seven verses of chapter 15, the will of God in regard to the believer's relation to those who are weak in the faith.

We note, then, that the believer is here looked upon as a member of the Body of Christ, and this while speaking of wondrous privilege, nevertheless involves grave responsibility. It might be well to point out here that the Body of Christ is looked at in two very distinct aspects in the epistles. In Ephesians and Colossians we have the Body in its dispensational aspect, embracing all believers from Pentecost to the return of the Lord for His Church. Looked at in this way, Christ alone is the Head, and all are united to Him, whether as to their actual condition they be numbered among the living or the dead. But in 1 Corinthians 12, and here in Romans 12, the Body is looked upon as something manifested on the earth, and therefore the apostle speaks of eyes, and ears, etc., as in the body here below. The absurd deduction has been drawn from this that the *Church* of the book of Acts and of the early epistles of Paul is not at all the same thing as the Church of the prison epistles. This view is pure assumption, based upon a far-fetched dispensationalism that destroys a sense of Christian responsibility to a very large degree wherever it is fully embraced. In Corinthians, and in Romans, too, the Body of Christ is viewed on earth; and inasmuch as there are those set in the Church who speak and act for the Head in heaven, it is quite in keeping to use the figures of the eyes, ears, and so on. "If one member suffer, all the members suffer with it," could not be said of saints in heaven. Their sufferings are forever over; but as long as there is a suffering saint on earth, every other member of the Body of Christ shares with him in his affliction.

I remember well, as a boy, gazing with rapt admiration upon a regiment of Highlanders as they marched through the streets of my native city, Toronto, Canada, and I was thrilled when I was told that that regiment had fought in the battle of Waterloo. It was quite a disappointment to me afterwards to learn that not one man of them all had been in that great battle. I was gazing on the regiment as then constituted, and the battle of Waterloo had taken place many years before; but it was the same regiment, new recruits taking the places constantly of those who passed away. So it is with the Body of Christ on earth. Believers die and depart to be with Christ and join the choir invisible above; others take their places here below, and thus the Church continues from century to century.

Now as a member of Christ's Body I need to realize that I am not to act independently of other members; nor am I to think of myself as exalted above the rest, but to think soberly as one to whom God has dealt a measure of faith, as He also has to every other Christian. As there are many members in the human body, and no two members have the same office, so believers, though many together constitute one Body in Christ, and are all members, one of another. But our gifts differ, and each one is to use whatever gifts may be given to him according to the grace that God supplies. If he have the gift of prophecy, he is to speak according to the proportion of faith; if his place be characteristically that of service, let him serve in subjection to the Lord; if he be a teacher, let him teach in lowly grace; if an ex-horter, let him seek to stir up his brethren, but in the love of Christ; if he be one to whom God has entrusted earthly treasure, that he may give generously to relieve the need of his brethren or to further the work of the gospel, let him dis-tribute with simplicity, not ostentatiously as drawing attention to himself, or his gifts; if he be fitted to rule in the assembly of God let him be a diligent pastor, or shepherd of the flock; if it be given him to show mercy to the needy, or undeserving, let it be with cheerfulness.

Above all things, let *love* be genuine, without pretence or hypocrisy, abhorring that which is evil but cleaving to that which is good.

How much we need the simple exhortations of verse 10: "Be kindly affectioned one to another with brotherly love; in honor preferring one another."

Elsewhere he writes: "Be ye kind one to another." How rare a virtue true kindness is! How often pretended zeal for truth, or for Church position, dries up the milk of human kindness! And yet this is one of the truest Christian virtues. Dr. Griffith Thomas used to tell of an old Scotch pastor who frequently said to his congregation: "Remember, if you are not very kind, you are not very spiritual." And yet how often people imagine that there is something even incongruous between spirituality and kindness! How differently would Christians speak of one another and act toward one another if these admonitions were but kept in view.

The first part of the eleventh verse is better translated, "Not remiss in zeal." It is not to be taken as a mere exhortation to careful business methods, but whatever one has to do should be done zealously, with spiritual fervor, as serving the Lord.

It is hardly necessary to take up each verse in detail. The exhortations are too plain to be misunderstood. In verse 16, however, it may be as well to point out that the apostle is not really inculcating condescension, as though of higher beings to those of less worth, but what he really says is: "Mind not high things, but go along with the lowly." The last five verses possibly have the world in view rather than fellow-Christians, and yet it is unhappily true that even in all dealings with fellow-believers the same admonitions are needed. It is not always possible to live peaceably, even with fellow-saints, let alone with men of the world. Therefore the word, *"If possible, as much lieth in you, live peaceably with all men."* Some have had difficulty over the meaning of the expression, "Give place unto wrath," in verse 19. What I understand the apostle to say is this: "Do not attempt to avenge yourselves, but leave room for the judgment of God. If wrath *must* be meted out, let Him do it, not yourself," for it it written: "Vengeance is Mine: I will repay, saith the Lord."

Savonarola said, "A Christian's life consists in doing good and suffering evil." It is not for him to take matters into his own hands, but rather to act upon verses 20 and 21, in simple confidence that God will not suffer any trial to come upon him through others which will not eventually work out for good.

This is not natural, but it is possible to the man
who walks in the Spirit. A young nobleman com-
plained to Francis of Assissi of a thief. "The
rascal," he cried, "has stolen my boots." "Run
after him quickly," exclaimed Francis, "and give
him your socks." This was the spirit of the
Lord Jesus "who when He was reviled, reviled not
again," and for hatred ever gave love.

No one can fail to see how like are these exhortations to the teaching of our blessed Lord,
in the so-called Sermon on the Mount. Yet the
difference is immense. For there His words were
the acid test of discipleship while waiting for
the coming of the kingdom which is yet to be displayed. But here we have exhortation to walk in
accord with the new nature which we possess
as children of God. It is not in order that we
"may be the children of our Father in heaven."
It is the manifestation of the Spirit's work in
those who belong to the new creation.

LECTURE XI

The Will of God as to the Believer's Relation to Government and to Society; and the Closing Sections

Chapters 13-16.

The position of the Christian in this world is necessarily, under the present order of things, a peculiarly difficult and almost anomalous one. He is a citizen of another world, passing as a stranger and a pilgrim through a strange land. Presumably loyal in heart to the rightful King, whom earth rejected and counted worthy only of a malefactor's cross, he finds himself called upon to walk in a godly and circumspect way in a scene of which Satan, the usurper, is the prince and god. Yet he is not to be an anarchist, nor is he to flaunt the present order of things. His rule ever should be: "We must obey God rather than man." Nevertheless he is not to be found in opposition to human government, even though the administrators of that government may be men of the most unrighteous type. As we come to the study of this thirteenth chapter, it is well for us to remember that he who sat upon the throne of empire when Paul gave this instruction concerning obedience to the powers that be, was one

of the vilest beasts in human form whoever occupied a throne—a sensuous, sensual brute, who
ripped up the body of his own mother in order
that he might see the womb that bore him—an
evil, blatant egotist of most despicable character,
whose cruelties and injustices beggar all descrip-
tion. And yet God in His providence permitted
this demon-controlled wretch to wear the diadem
of the greatest empire the world had yet known.
Paul himself designates him elsewhere as a savage
beast, when he writes to the young preacher
Timothy, "God delivered me out of the mouth
of the lion." While the powers of the emperor
were more or less circumscribed by the laws and
the Senate, nevertheless his rule was one that
could not but spell ruin and disaster for many of
the early Christians. What faith was required on
their part to obey the instruction given by the
Spirit of God in the first seven verses of this chapter! And if under such government Christians
were called upon to be obedient, surely there is no
place for sedition, or rebellion, under any government. "The potsherds of the earth may strive
with the potsherds of the earth," and one government may be overthrown by another; but whichever government is established in power at a given
time, the Christian is to be subject to it. He has
the resource of prayer if its edicts are tyrannous
and unjust, but he is not to rise in rebellion against
it. This is a hard saying for some of us, I know,

but if any be in doubt let him read carefully the verses now before us. "Let every soul be subject unto the higher powers. For there is no power but of God: the powers that be are ordained of God" (Ver.1).

This is not to seek to establish the doctrine of the divine right of kings, but it simply means this: That God, who sets up one man and puts down another for His own infinitely wise purpose, ordains that certain forms of government or certain rulers shall be in the place of authority at a given time. As the book of Daniel tells us, He sets over the nations the basest of men at times as a punishment for their wickedness; but in any case, there could be no authority if not providentially permitted and therefore recognized by Himself. To resist this authority, the second verse shows us, is to resist a divine ordinance. But it would certainly be far-fetched to say that they that resist shall receive to themselves damnation, if by "damnation" we mean everlasting punishment. The word here, as in Corinthians 11, means *judgment,* but not in the sense of eternal judgment necessarily. Rulers are not a terror to good works, but to the evil. Even a Nero respected such as walked in obedience to the law. The reason he persecuted the Christians was that they were reported to be opposed to existing institutions. He, then, who would not be afraid of those in authority is called upon to walk in obedience to the law— to do good, and thus his righteousness will be recognized; for, after all, the ruler is the minister of God to each one for good. But he who does evil, violating the institutions of the realm, may well fear, for into the magistrate's hand has been committed by God Himself, the sword, which he does not bear in vain, and he is set by God to be His minister in the government of the world and to execute judgment upon those who act in a criminal way. So, then, the Christian is called upon to be subject to government, not only to avoid condemnation, but also that he may himself maintain a good conscience toward God. Let him pay tribute, even though at times the demands may seem to be unrighteous, rendering to all their dues, paying his taxes honorably, and thus showing that he desires in all things to be subject to the government.

It will be observed that all the instruction we have here puts the Christian in the place of subjection, and not of authority; but, if in the providence of God, he be born to the purple, or put in the place of authority, he, too, is to be bound by the word of God as here set forth.

The balance of the chapter has to do with the Christian's relation to society in general, and that in view of the coming of the Lord and the soon-closing up of the present dispensation. He is to maintain the attitude not of a debtor but a giver; to owe no man anything, but rather to let love flow out freely to all. For every moral precept of the second table of the law, which sets forth man's duty to his neighbor, is summed up in the words: "Thou shalt love thy neighbor as thyself." He who thus loves could, by no possibility, ever be guilty of adultery, murder, theft, lying, or covetousness. It is impossible that love should be manifested in such ways as these. "Love worketh no ill to his neighbor: therefore love is the fulfilling of the law." It is in this way that the righteous requirement of the law is fulfilled in us who walk, not after the flesh, but after the Spirit, as we have already seen in looking at Chapter 8:1-4.

Every passing day brings the dispensation of grace nearer to its end and hastens the return of the Lord. It is not for the Christian, then, to be sleeping among the dead, but to be fully awake to his responsibilities and privileges, realizing that the salvation for which we wait—the redemption of the body—is nearer now than when we believed. The night when Satan's sway bears rule over the earth has nearly drawn to its close. Already the light of day begins to dawn. It is not, therefore, for those who have been saved by grace to have aught to do with works of darkness, but rather, as soldiers, to have on the armor of light, standing for that which is of God, living incorruptly as in the full light of day, not in debauchery or wantonness of any kind, neither in strife and envying; but having put on the Lord Jesus

Christ, having confessed themselves as one with Him, to take the place of death with Him in a practical sense, thus making no provision for the indulgence of the lust of the flesh. It was these two closing verses of this thirteenth chapter that spoke so loudly to the heart of Augustine of Hippo when, after years of distress, he was fearful to confess Christ openly, even when intellectually convinced that he should be a Christian, lest he would find himself unable to hold his carnal nature in subjection, and so might bring grave discredit upon the cause with which he thought of identifying himself. But as he read the words: "Let us walk honestly, as in the day; not in rioting and drunkenness, not in chambering and wantonness, not in strife and envying; but put ye on the Lord Jesus Christ, and make not provision for the flesh, to fulfil the lusts thereof" the Spirit of God opened his eyes to see that the power for victory was not in himself, but in the fact that he was identified with a crucified and risen Saviour.

As he gazed by faith upon His blessed face and the Holy Spirit showed him something of the truth of union with Christ, he entered into the assurance of salvation and realized victory over sin. When in an unexpected way he came face to face with one of the beautiful but wanton companions of his former days, he turned and ran. She followed, crying, "Austin, Austin, why do you run? It is only I." He replied as he sped on his way, "I run, because it is not I!" Thus he made no provision for the flesh.

In chapter 14 and the first seven verses of chapter 15 the Holy Spirit emphasizes the believer's responsibilities toward his weaker brethren. He is to walk charitably toward those who have less light than himself.

The weak in faith, that is, those whose uninstructed consciences cause them to be in trouble as to things indifferent, are to be received and owned as in this full Christian position and not to be judged for their questionings or doubtful thoughts. The principle is a most far-reaching one, and indicates the breadth of Christian charity that should prevail over the spirit of legality into which it is so easy to fall. Light is not the ground of reception to Christian privileges, but life. All those who are children of God are to be recognized as fellow-members of the Body, and unless living in evident wickedness, to be accorded their blood-bought place in the Christian company. Wickedness and weakness are not to be confounded. The wicked person is to be put away (see 1 Cor. 5), but the weak brother is to be received and protected.

Of course it is not reception into fellowship that is here in view. The one who was weak in faith was already inside. He must not be looked upon coldly and judged for his doubtful thoughts (see margin), but received cordially, and his weak con-

science carefully considered. It might be one who
is still under law as to things clean and unclean
or one who has difficulty regarding holy days.
In the former case the brother who is strong in
the liberty that is in Christ believes he may, as a
Christian, eat all things, raising no questions as
to their ceremonial cleanness. The weak brother
is so afraid of defilement he subsists on a vegetable
diet rather than possibly partake of what has
been offered to idols or is not "Kosher"—that is,
clean according to Levitical law.

The one who is "strong" must not look with con-
tempt upon his over-scrupulous brother. On the
other hand, the weak one is forbidden to accuse
the stronger of insincerity or inconsistency.

Or if it be a question of days and one brother
with a legal conscience possibly still holds to the
sanctity of the Jewish Sabbath, while another sees
all days as now alike and to be devoted to the glory
of God, each must seek to act as before Him and
be "fully persuaded in his own mind."

Who has given one servant to regulate another?
Both are accountable to one Master, and He rec-
ognizes integrity of heart, and will uphold His
own. Where there is sincerity and it is the glory
of the Lord that each has in view, both must endeavor to act as in His presence. There can be no
question but that the principle here enunciated if
firmly held would make for fuller fellowship among
saints and save from many heart-burnings.

We do not live for ourselves. Whether we will or no we are constantly affecting others for good or ill. Let us then recognize our individual responsibility to the Lord, whose we are and whom we are to serve, whether in life or in death. "For to this end Christ both died and rose that He might be Lord both of the dead and living." The words, "and revived," are a needless interpolation omitted from all critical versions.

At the judgment-seat of God (according to the best reading), where Christ Himself is the Arbiter, all will come out, and He will show what was in accord with His mind. Till then we can afford to wait, realizing that we must all give account of ourselves to Him. In view of this, "Let us not judge one another any more," but let there be individual self-judgment, each one striving so to walk as not to put any occasion to fall in a weak brother's way.

Even where one is clear that his own behavior is consistent with Christian liberty, let him not flaunt that liberty before the weak lest he "destroy one for whom Christ died." See also 1 Cor. 8:11. It is of course the ruin of his testimony that is in view. Emboldened by the example of the strong one he may venture to go beyond the dictates of conscience and so bring himself under a sense of condemnation, or he may become discouraged, thinking others inconsistent, and so drift from the Christian company.

After all, questions of meats and drinks are but of minor importance. "For the kingdom of God is not meat and drink"—i. e., has not to do with temporalities as have all merely human kingdoms—but it is spiritual in character and has to do with "righteousness, peace, and joy in the Holy Spirit." Where one is exercised as to these things (even though mistaken as to others) he serves Christ, and is acceptable to God and approved of men.

Every right-thinking person appreciates sincerity. "Let us therefore follow after the things that make for peace, and things wherewith one may edify another."

It is far better to abstain from ought that would trouble the conscience of a weak brother than to turn him aside by insisting on liberty, and so be responsible for his failure and the break-down of his discipleship.

If one has faith that he can safely do what another condemns, let him have it to himself before God and not flaunt it flagrantly before the weak. But let him be sure he is not self-condemned while he professes to be clear; for he who persists in a certain course concerning which he is not really at ease before God does not truly act in faith, and so is condemned (not "damned" of course—for this word properly refers to eternal judgment), because "whatsoever is not of faith is sin." That is to say, if I act contrary to what I believe to be right,

even though there be nothing morally wrong in
my behavior, I am really sinning against conscience and thus against God.

He sums it all up in the first seven verses of
chapter 15. The strong should bear the burdens
of the weak—as sympathetically entering into
their difficulties—and not insist on liberty to please
themselves. Rather let each one have his neighbor's good in view, seeking his building up and not
carelessly destroying his faith by ruthlessly insisting on his own personal liberty. True liberty
will be manifested by refraining from what would
stumble a weaker one.

In this Christ is the great example. He who
need never have yielded to any legal enactment,
voluntarily submitted to every precept of the law,
and even went far beyond it, pleasing not Himself
(as when He paid the temple tax, giving as His
reason, "Lest we should stumble them"), thus
taking upon Himself the reproaches of those who
reproached God. His outward behavior was as
blameless as His inward life, yet men reviled Him
as they reviled God.

Verse 4 stresses the importance of Old Testament Scripture. "Whatsoever things were written
aforetime were written for our learning, that we
through patience and comfort of the Scriptures
might have hope." Link with this 1 Cor. 10:6, 11.
"All Scripture is not about me, but all Scripture is
for me." is a quotation well worth remembering.

He closes this section by praying that "the God of patience and consolation" may give the saints to be of one mind toward each other, with Christ whose blessed example he has cited, that all may unitedly glorify God, even the Father of our Lord Jesus Christ. Mind and mouth must be in agreement if this be so. And so he exhorts them to receive one another as Christ also received us to the glory of God. If Christ could take us up in grace— whether weak or strong—and make us meet for the glory, surely we can be cordial and Christ-like in our fellowship one with another. Again, I repeat, it is not the question of receiving into the Christian company that is in view here, but the recognition of those already inside.

Properly speaking the epistle as such—the treatise on the righteousness of God—is brought to a conclusion in verses 8-13. All that comes afterwards is more in the nature of postscript and appendix.

What has really been demonstrated in this very full treatise? "Now I say that Jesus Christ was a minister of the circumcision for the truth of God, to confirm the promises made unto the fathers: and that the Gentiles might glorify God for His mercy." That is, he has shown throughout that our Lord came in full accord with the Old Testament promises. He entered into the sheepfold by the door (as John's Gospel tells us in Chap. 10), and was the divinely appointed minister to the

Jews, come to confirm the covenanted promises. Though the nation rejected Him this does not invalidate His ministry but it opens the door of mercy to the Gentiles in a wider way than ever, though in full accord with the Jewish Scriptures. And so he cites passage after passage to clinch the truth already taught so clearly, that it was foreknown and predetermined that the Gentiles should hear the gospel and be given the same opportunity to be saved that the Jew enjoyed. That this "mercy" actually transcends anything revealed in past ages we know since "the revelation of the mystery," to which he alludes in the last verses of the next chapter. But his point here is that it is not contrary to the predictions of the prophets, but entirely consistent with what God had been pleased to make known beforehand. And so he brings this masterly unfolding of the gospel and its result to a close by saying, "Now the God of hope fill you with all joy and peace in believing, that ye may abound in hope, through the power of the Holy Spirit" (vs. 13). In believing what? Why, simply in believing the great truths set forth in the epistle—the tremendous verities of our most holy faith—setting before us man's ruin by sin and his redemption through Christ Jesus. When we believe this we are filled with joy and peace as we look on in hope to the consummation of it all at our Lord's return, meantime walking before God in the power of the indwelling Spirit who alone makes these precious things real to us.

The balance of the chapter takes on a distinctly personal character as the apostle takes the saints at Rome into his confidence and tells them of his exercises regarding them and his purpose to visit them. From the reports that had come to him he was persuaded that they were already in a very healthy spiritual state, "full of goodness, filled with all knowledge, and able also to admonish one another," so he had no thought of going to them as a regulator but he felt that he had a ministry, committed to him by God which would be profitable for them; and, besides, Rome was part of that great Gentile world into which he had been sent and to which his ministry specially applied, "that the offering up of the Gentiles might be acceptable, being sanctified by the Holy Spirit." Israel was no longer the one separate nation but the gospel was for all alike.

It was therefore to be expected that he should visit them whenever the way was opened, and as it seemed to him that his mission to those in Asia Minor and eastern Europe was now in large measure fulfilled, he purposed shortly going westward as far as to Spain and hoped to visit them on the way. Meantime he was going up to Jerusalem to carry an offering from the saints of Macedonia and Achaia to the needy believers of Judea. As soon as this was accomplished he hoped to leave

for Spain visiting them en route. What a mercy
that the near future was sealed to him. How
little he realized what he must soon be called upon
to suffer for Christ's name's sake. "Man proposes,
but God disposes." And He had quite other plans
for His devoted servant—though they included
a visit to Rome, but in chains!

Sure that in God's due time he would get to
them and "come in the fulness of the blessing of
the gospel of Christ," he beseeches them to pray
for the success of his mission to his own country-
men and that he might be delivered from the unbelieving Jews. The prayer was answered, but in
how different a manner to what he anticipated!

Chapter 16 consists largely of salutations to
saints known to him, now dwelling in Rome, and
from others who were in his company. The first
two verses are in the nature of a letter of commendation for Phoebe a deaconess of the assembly in Cenchrea, a town just south of Corinth, in
Achaia (see Acts 18:18). She would doubtless be
well-known to Aquila and Priscilla (who are mentioned by name—in inverse order—in the next
verse) but he does not leave her to depend upon
her friends' recollections of the past, but by this
letter assures the saints of her present standing in
the Church.

Priscilla and Aquila were to him as members of
his own family—so intimate had been their association; and he cannot forget how they had put

themselves in jeopardy for his sake. It was in their house that one of the assemblies in Rome met. Another of the saints from Achaia was there also, Epaenetus, firstfruits of his mission to Corinth.

As we go over the long list and note the delicate touches, the tender recollections, the slight differences in commendation, we feel we are drawn very close to these early believers, and we would like to know more of their history and experiences. We are interested in learning that there were relatives of his, Andronicus and Junia, who, he says, were "in Christ before me," and we wonder if their prayers for their brilliant young kinsman may not have had much to do with his remarkable conversion.

Another kinsman is mentioned in verse 11, Herodion by name, but whether converted before or after him we are not told.

There is a very human touch in the 13th verse. "Salute Rufus, chosen in the Lord, and his mother and mine." Somewhere on his journeys this Christian matron, though unnamed, had mothered the devoted and self-denying servant of Christ, and he remembered with a peculiar gratitude her care for him.

All the names are of interest, and we shall be glad to meet them all "in that day," and learn more of their devotion to the Lord and their suf-

ferings for His Name's sake, though we cannot
linger over the record here.

Before sending messages from his associates he
puts in a warning word against false teachers, in
verses 17 and 18. "Now I beseech you, brethren,
mark them which cause divisions and offences contrary to the doctrine which ye have learned, and
avoid them. For they that are such serve not our
Lord Jesus Christ, but their own belly, and by
good words and fair speeches deceive the hearts
of the simple." The evil-doers here referred to are
not Christian teachers, even though in error. They
are ungodly men who, as Jude tells us, have crept
in from the outside. They are not servants of
Christ but tools of the devil, brought in from the
world to corrupt and divide the people of God. It
is a fearfully wicked thing to apply such words to
real Christians who, however mistaken they may,
be, love the Lord and yearn over His people, de-
siring their blessing. In Phil. 3:18, 19 we learn
more of those "who serve their own belly," that
is, who live only for self-gratification. "Many
walk, of whom I have told you often, and now tell
you even weeping, that they are the enemies of
the cross of Christ; whose end is destruction,
whose God is their belly, and whose glory is
in their shame, who mind earthly things."
These are identical with the wretched divi-
sion-makers of our present chapter. Let us
be exceedingly careful how we charge true servants

of Christ with being of this unholy number, even
though we may feel that truth compels us to take
issue with them as to some things they do or teach.

Though he warns the Roman saints of the danger of listening to men of this type he lets them
know that he has only heard good things of them,
but he is jealous that they should maintain their
excellent record.   Alas, how soon did this very
Church open its doors to just such false teachers
as he warned them against, and so by the seventh
century you have the Papacy itself enthroned in
Rome!

He would have us simple concerning evil and
wise unto what is good, not occupied with error
but with truth.   That truth will triumph soon
when the God of peace shall bruise Satan under
the feet of the saints.

The closing salutations from Paul and his companions are given in verses 21-24.   Timothy and
Luke were with him.   We now learn for the first
time that Jason was a near relative (see Acts
17:5-9), which accounts in measure for his reception of and devotion to Paul upon the visit to
Thessalonica.   Sosipater, also a kinsman, is linked
with him.

Tertius, the scribe who acted as Paul's aman-
uensis, adds his greeting.   Apart from this we
should never have known the name of the actual
writer of the letter.

Was the "Gaius mine host," of verse 23, the same as the Gaius who received the travelling brethren and was commended by John for his Christian hospitality, in his 3rd epistle? We do not know, but he was at least a man of the same spirit. Of Erastus we have heard elsewhere (Acts 19:22; 2 Tim. 4:20), but Quartus is not mentioned in any other passage. Both the names Tertius and Quartus would indicate that those who bore them were probably slaves at one time—their names just meaning the third and the fourth respectively. Slaves were often named simply by number.

The benediction of verse 24 concludes the epistle and marks it as genuinely Pauline. See 2 Thess. 3:17,18. "Grace" was his secret mark, so to speak, that attested his authorship. Significantly enough it is found in Hebrews 13:25, and in no other epistles save in his.

Verses 25 to 27 are an appendix, in which he links his precious unfolding of the gospel with that "mystery" which it was his special province to make known among the Gentiles, and which is unfolded so fully in Eph. 3 and several other scriptures.

"Now to Him that is of power to establish you according to my gospel and the preaching of Jesus Christ, according to the revelation of the mystery which was kept secret since the ages began, but now is made manifest, and by pro-

phetic writings, according to the commandment
of the everlasting God, made known to all nations
for the obedience of faith; to God only wise be
glory through Jesus Christ forever. Amen."

To Paul was committed a two-fold ministry—
that of the gospel (as linked with a glorified
Christ) and that of the Church—the mystery hid
in God from before the creation of the world but
now revealed by the Spirit. See this double ministry as set forth in Col 1:23-29 and Eph. 3:1-12.

"The mystery" was not something of difficult,
mysterious character, but a sacred secret never
known to mankind until in due time opened up
by the Holy Spirit through the apostle Paul, and
by him communicated to all nations for the obedience of faith. It was not hid in the Scriptures to
be brought to light eventually; but we are distinctly told it was hid in God until such time as
He chose to manifest it. This was not until Israel
had been given every opportunity to receive Christ
both in incarnation and resurrection. When they
definitely refused Him God made known what had
been in His heart from eternity—that from all
nations, Jews and Gentiles, He would redeem and
take out an elect company who would, by the
Spirit's baptism, be formed into one Body to be
associated with Christ, in the most intimate relationship (likened in Eph. 5 to that of husband
and wife, or head and body), not only now but
through all the ages to come.

This great mystery of Christ and the Church has now been manifested and made known by prophetic writings—not as translated here "by the Scriptures of the prophets"—but the meaning clearly is, made known by the writings of inspired men, New Testament prophets, in this day of gospel light and testimony.

Nor is it just a beautiful and wonderful theory or system of doctrine to be held in the intellect. It involves present identification with Christ in His rejection, and hence is made known to all nations for the obedience of faith. It is not developed in the epistle to the Romans, for here the great theme, as we have seen, is the Righteousness of God as revealed in the Gospel. But it is touched on here in order to link the unfolding of the gospel in this letter with the revelation of the mystery, as given in the prison epistles particularly. This is not to say that we have new and higher truth in Ephesians and Colossians, for instance, than in Romans and earlier letters. All form part of one whole, and constitute that body of teaching everywhere proclaimed by the apostle through his long years of ministry, but not all committed to writing at one time. The "mystery" of Romans 16:25 is the same as that of the later epistles, and ever formed an integral part of his messages. It would not be necessary to say this were there not some to-day who would divorce completely Paul's ministry in

Acts from that which he embodied in the last of his letters written after the rejection of his message by the Jews in Rome as recorded in Acts 28. The appendix to the Roman letter is the complete denial of this. It is here added to manifest the unity of his ministry of the gospel and the Church, through two-fold in character.

And with this we conclude our present somewhat cursory study, trusting that our review of the epistle has not been in vain, but will be for increased profit and blessing as we wait for God's Son from heaven.

"To God only wise be glory through Jesus Christ for ever. Amen."